MAIDSTONE
A HISTORY

MAIDSTONE
A HISTORY

Cyril Cooper

Phillimore

MAP

OF THE TOWN OF

MAIDSTONE

IN THE COUNTY OF

KENT,

1848.

PUBLISHED BY J. TOOTELL, SURVEYOR, MAIDSTONE.

Scale of Chains

2008, reprinted 2010

Published by
PHILLIMORE & CO. LTD
Andover, Hampshire, England
www.phillimore.co.uk

ISBN 978-1-86077-648-9

Printed and bound in Great Britain.
Manufacturing managed by Jellyfish Print Solutions Ltd.

Contents

LIST OF ILLUSTRATIONS

ACKNOWLEDGEMENTS

All illustrations have been kindly supplied by Maidstone Museum and Art Gallery, except:

Centre for Kentish Studies, 69; Cyril Cooper, 3, 5, 15, 25, 45, 62, 64, 79-80, 127-8, 137; *Kent Messenger*, 123-5, 134, 138-41; Dr Bob Spain, 39.

My interest in Kentish history was encouraged by Drs Elizabeth Edwards and Grayson Ditchfield and the academic staff of the History Department of the University of Kent. The present endeavour has been greatly assisted by Giles Guthrie, Keeper of Human History at Maidstone Museum, Fiona Woolley, Keeper of Fine and Applied Art at the Bentlif Art Gallery, and Barry Hollis, Picture Services Editor of The *Kent Messenger* Group. Finally, I should mention the considerable help and suggestions which I have had from Simon Thraves and Sarah Pavey of Phillimore, the Publisher of Local History. I am very grateful to all of them.

INTRODUCTION

Maidstone is in the Lower Medway Valley and had a population of 138,948 at the time of the 2001 Census. There are two major histories of the town, Russell's *History of Maidstone* (1881), which remains a useful reference, and Clark and Murfin's *The History of Maidstone: The Making of a Modern County Town* (1995). In a short history such as this it is necessary to be selective, so what I have set out to do is to include a number of events of historical importance which have not been dealt with at all, or only in passing, in earlier histories. From Roman times onwards, the present history deals principally with the town of Maidstone rather than the extended borough which now exists.

Close to what is now the town of Maidstone there is evidence, in the form of mammalian remains, of the Palaeolithic period (from 3,000,000 years ago until about 12000 B.C.). The national Geological Survey collection contains remains of iguanodon, deer, horse, hippopotamus, hyena, elephant and rhinoceros from the earlier part of this period. Homo sapiens made an appearance in the area in the Mesolithic period (12000-3000 B.C.), as is evidenced by the many Stone-Age implements which have been found.

Only three to five miles from the present-day town are the Neolithic (4000-2400 B.C.) Medway megaliths, unique in eastern England.

At the end of the 13th century, the Archbishop of Canterbury was intent on making Maidstone a principal centre of English Christianity. Although building for this purpose had commenced, the project was frustrated by a veto of Henry III, but had it proceeded it is possible that Maidstone might have replaced Canterbury as the centre of the Christian Church.

Maidstone and the surrounding district were centres of industry from Roman times, beginning with quarrying of ragstone and tile making and going through periods of fulling of wool, weaving, threadmaking, papermaking, engineering and brewing. Agriculture, particularly fruit and hop growing, played an important part in the life of the town, as did the river until road transport took over. By the mid-20th century industry on any large scale had come to an end and now, as in many county towns, service industries and retailing have taken over.

A feature of Maidstone which makes it almost unique in south-eastern England is the extent to

1 *The iguanodon quarry near Oakwood, now the garden of a private house, in which prehistoric skeletons were discovered in 1834.*

which rebellions and revolts against authority either began here or involved local townspeople. Maidstone men were much involved in the Peasant's Revolt of 1381 and, although it cannot be said with certainty, it is thought its leaders came from the area. Townsfolk took an active part in Jack Cade's rebellion of 1450 and the town eventually received a royal pardon for the part which it had played in that episode. Some thirty years later the Duke of Buckingham's

unsuccessful plot to replace Richard III by Henry VII was planned at the Mote and large numbers of rebels were mustered on Penenden Heath. The Wyatt rebellion of 1554, designed to frustrate the marriage of Mary I and Philip of Spain, was widely supported in Maidstone and the campaign began there.

In 1648 the Battle of Maidstone took place between a Parliamentary force numbering some 4,000 and, perhaps, an equal number of Royalist supporters. The latter were heavily defeated, with 300 dead, whilst the Parliamentarians suffered 80 casualties. Not all Maidstone men were Royalist supporters, though, and the Mayor played a leading role in the trial and execution of Charles I. Towards the end of the 18th century the townspeople were opposed to the Revolutionary War against France, the legislation against treason and sedition, and the suspension of Habeas Corpus by the government of Pitt the Younger. They were, nevertheless, patriotic and there was no difficulty in raising a Volunteer unit to assist in the defence of the country if need be.

The Swing Riots in 1830 were a manifestation of agricultural discontent and, in the main, limited in Kent to the countryside. Of Kentish towns, only Maidstone was directly affected, a principal leader of the riots in West Kent being a Maidstone shoemaker.

By the later 19th and early 20th centuries many of the old buildings had been demolished to make way for offices, shops and houses, although numbers remain including All Saints' Church, parts of the late 14th-century College buildings, Corpus Christi Hall, the Archbishop's Palace and what is now the Carriage Museum, and the house of Andrew Broughton, who played a leading role in the trial and execution of King Charles. The pattern of the High Street and the streets leading off it has remained largely unchanged over many hundreds of years, and several Tudor buildings are still to be seen in their original condition, although not all are immediately recognisable from street level, their exteriors having been altered.

ONE

From Earliest Times to the Fourteenth Century

Apart from a passing reference in *Textus Roffensis* of around A.D. 975, in which the manor of Maidstone is recorded as being in the possession of the Archbishop of Canterbury, there are no written records of Maidstone prior to Domesday Book. Until then we have to rely on archaeological evidence of human habitation in the Lower Medway valley, which includes the area that is now the town of Maidstone. There is a history of scattered habitation extending back to Neolithic times (7000B.P.), flint implements and stone axes having been discovered in the town and the immediate surrounding area. On the eastern side of the River Medway near Aylesford, some three miles from Maidstone, there are well-known megaliths from the third or second millennium B.C., and there are others on the western side near Addington, some five miles away. These are the only megaliths in eastern England, which provides some indication that the area was of importance even at this early period. There have been finds of Bronze-Age material in Maidstone itself and in the surrounding area, whilst gold ornaments have been recovered from the lower reaches of the Medway.

By the time of the Roman invasion Maidstone had acquired importance as a trading and communications centre. The Medway provided access to the Thames and thus to London, whilst earlier droving trackways down to the Weald ran broadly from north to south in the area of Maidstone. An important highway (Stone Street) led from Rochester and Watling Street to Maidstone and thence to the iron workings towards the south of the county and onwards to Hastings. There was a substantial Roman-type villa at the Mount built in the middle to late second century, situated parallel to the river and not far from the present East railway station, which was occupied well into the fourth century. It is probable that the villa belonged to a native landowner rather than to a Roman official since there is no evidence in Maidstone during the Roman period of any settlement other than farmsteads or scattered dwellings. There are indications of other Roman-type villas at Florence Street and Barton Road, and it is probable that the remains at several other sites in the borough are of the same period. There is evidence to support the proposition that the Roman villa at Eccles near Maidstone was re-used in Anglo-Saxon times but this is the known extent of early Anglo-Saxon occupation of the area.

Further evidence of habitation was found in the inhumation burials at Wheeler Street containing weapons and other artefacts which have been dated to the first century. A third- or fourth-century walled cemetery was discovered in the West Borough, at a location between the old boys' grammar school and the West railway station, where there had been some 150 cremations and up to 30 inhumations. Eight burials were located by excavations at the Fremlin Walk site and these have been dated from the late Iron Age to the third century.

Maidstone was of sufficient importance to be included in Domesday Book:

> The archbishop holds Meddestane. It answers for ten sulings [around 2,000 acres]. Land for 30 ploughs. In lordship 3 ploughs. 25 villagers with 21 smallholders have 25 ploughs. A church; 10 slaves; five mills at 36s. 8d.; 2 fisheries at 270 eels. Meadow, 10 acres; woodland, 30 pigs.
> Of this manor three men-at-arms hold four sulings from the Archbishop; they have 3½ ploughs in lordship, and 32 villagers with ten smallholders who have 6 ploughs. 10 vassals. They (also) have 1 mill at 5s.; meadow, 13 acres; 2½ fisheries at 180 eels; 2 salt-houses; woodland, 23 pigs.
> Total value of this manor before 1066 £14; when acquired £12; now the value of the Archbishop's lordship £20; the men-at-arms' £15 10s.
> The monks of Canterbury have 20s. from 2 men of this manor every year.

Every Easter the Archbishop was in receipt of a quantity of honey, eight lambs, 60 loaves, 12d. for wine and 14d. for oil from his Maidstone manor.

The villagers and smallholders of Maidstone totalled 88 householders, and in addition there were 20 vassals. There may have been sub-tenants and there would certainly have been landless peasants. Small numbers would have been employed at the saltworks, the mills and fisheries. It is not possible to deduce the population at this time, but there may have been as many as 100 houses scattered around the manor.

There can be no certainty when the church of St Mary's, to which Domesday must refer, was built but it may well have been in the eighth century. It was a minster church and the priests and their households would have resided as a community around the church, which is most likely to have been situated where or near where All Saints' now stands. The church was recorded in an archiepiscopal survey in 1070 as one of the most important and wealthy churches in Kent. In 1291 the papal taxation shows that it was taxed at £106 13s. 4d., more than any other church in the diocese except for Minster and Reculver. John Mansell, a rector who died in 1264, held, according to Edward Hasted, a remarkable collection of royal offices. He was Chief Justice of England, a member of the Privy Council, Keeper of the Great Seal and Ambassador to France. By the mid-13th century, or possible earlier, a second church, St Faith's, was built as a dependency of St Mary's.

Domesday records that Penenden Heath, part of present-day Maidstone, was established as the county meeting place. It served as the venue for the hundred court dealing with criminal matters for the area some distance around Maidstone, for the sheriff's court covering the whole of Kent and, from time to time, for the assizes attended by the royal justices. Those condemned to hanging by the Penenden courts suffered death on the Heath at the hands of the Archbishop's labourers.

2   *Archbishop's Palace viewed from Mill Street, 1868.*

In what was an episcopal manor it was natural that the church would play a dominant role. In Maidstone there was a manorial court, which would have been concerned with civil matters, possibly located on the site of the present Archbishop's Palace. The Archbishop had a gaol in the town in which heretics and excommunicants were confined. The governance of the town was in the hands of a portreeve, two ale-tasters and brethren, often numbering twelve. The officials were elected at annual meetings of the Archbishop's tenants, but for the office of portreeve two nominees were required and the Archbishop would choose one of them.

At the beginning of the 13th century the Archbishop was gifted the rectory by William de Cornhill, then rector of Maidstone. This was largely demolished in 1348 and replaced by a larger building. With further alterations and enlargements it had, by the following century,

become one of the Archbishop's principal residences. In the early 13th century Archbishop Edmund of Abingdon revived an earlier proposal to found a church of secular priests in Maidstone, principally to provide for the Canterbury clerks engaged in administration of the diocese. The idea was strongly resisted by the monks of Canterbury, who feared that it might lead to their losing the right to elect the Archbishop and even to the See being transferred away from Canterbury. They appealed to Pope Gregory IX who instructed Cardinal Otto, the papal legate, to conduct an enquiry and inspect the proposed site. The monks' appeal failed and in 1238 plans were drawn up by Elias of Dereham for a great church at Maidstone with fifty prebends. Building began in May 1239. The Christ Church monks made a further appeal to Henry III and were successful, and in November the Sheriff of Kent brought the project to an end.

3   *Archbishop's Stables, now the Museum of Carriages.*

In 1261 Archbishop Boniface founded, in the name of Saints Peter and Paul, a hospital designated 'le Newark' situated in the West Borough. It was intended not to heal the sick but to maintain ten poor men. The chaplain was the master of the hospital and the tithes of the chapels of East Farleigh, Linton and Sutton-by-Dover were apportioned to meet part of the costs of its upkeep. At about the same time that the hospital was built, Henry III granted to Archbishop Boniface a charter allowing a weekly market to be held on Thursdays, in addition to the market which was already being held on Sundays.

Archbishop Winchelsey was visiting the town in 1297 when he found himself besieged by armed men in Maidstone rectory. King Edward I had required a subsidy from the Church at large, but the Archbishop felt bound by a papal bull of Pope Boniface VIII forbidding churches from handing over property to the laity. The Archbishop agreed to consult with the Vatican on the matter but the King thereupon outlawed the clergy and took their goods, which they were able to recover only after making a monetary payment. Most complied but the Archbishop was one who refused. In January 1298 he ordered the rural dean of Sutton to inform the congregation at Mass that those men who had besieged him in the rectory had been excommunicated.

Maidstone was still principally a market town, with farmers providing foodstuffs and home-based craftsmen providing clothing, shoes and other necessities for the townsfolk and for those living nearby, but a small number of trades and industries dealt with a wider market. Stonemasons, for example, were involved in the quarrying and working of ragstone, and there was a quarry in the Willington Street area which had possibly been worked from the time of the Roman occupation. In later, unspecified, periods, there were underground workings at Mote Park, Spot Lane and Otham. The stone was used widely in south-east England, as well as for Queen Philippa's great wardrobe 'La Rioll', London Wall, the Palace of Westminster and other major projects in London.

There is evidence that in 1273, and possibly even earlier, the town attracted a small number of entrepreneurs who were dealing in large quantities of wool for export. Other middlemen, based in London, sent quantities of hides to Maidstone for processing, the tanned leather being returned for manufacture and marketing in London. Many housewives were engaged in the small-scale brewing of ale for both home consumption and for sale on market and fair days. When the roofs of the great barn and kitchen on the Christ Church manor at Hollingbourne were tiled in 1299-1300, materials were obtained from Maidstone. The kitchen alone required 20,440 tiles, but tiles for the barn itself were purchased more cheaply from Westwell. Some pottery was made in Maidstone, to meet both local demand and that of the London market.

By the 14th century access to the town had been significantly improved. The crossing over the Medway from the West Borough to the High Street had originally been by way of a ferry, but this was augmented, or perhaps replaced, by a

4 *The Horseway, a path between the church and college leading to a ford or ferry, was possibly in existence from prehistoric times.*

5 *Ragstone Quarry, Postley Road.*

6 *Eighteenth-century view of the bridge over the Medway.*

wooden bridge, which was in turn superseded by a stone bridge. The dates for these developments are not known with certainty, but it is probable that the stone bridge was erected in the 14th century. The markets, now readily accessible from towns and villages on either side of the river, became the largest and most important in the area, buyers and sellers of agricultural produce and household goods travelling to the town. In addition to the markets, there were four fairs held each year. These took place in February, May, June and October and were primarily for the sale of agricultural produce, but local craftsmen and tradesmen took the opportunity to offer their wares for sale.

In 1331 Edward III invited Flemish clothworkers to come to work in England.

John Kemp and some of his workmen set up trade in Cranbrook, clothmaking in Maidstone remaining insignificant until 1567, but Maidstone benefited indirectly from the development. The fulling process was essential to removing the natural grease from the wool and Maidstone and the surrounding area was ideal for this purpose, having clean water, numerous watermills, and fuller's earth, the necessary raw material. Fuller's earth was abundant enough to be exported from Maidstone to other parts of the country.

Ragstone was described as 'urnel', and in 1338 '400 stones of Maydenston called ournel' were bought for 22s. for work on the water-gate of the Tower of London, whilst in 1363, 650 feet of urnel was purchased to repair the walls of

7   View of Old Mill Street.

8   The weatherboarded Church Mill, demolished in 1902.

9　The Flour Mill and base of what was probably the earlier Archbishop's Mill, demolished in 1903.

10　Mill House, Mill Street.

the Tower, at a cost per one hundred feet, with freightage from Maidstone of 9s. Kentish rag was used for the College of Saint George at Windsor Castle, 100 stones called 'cobbels', each containing 3½ feet at 2d. a foot, being shipped from Maidstone.

The town remained relatively small in the 14th century. It was as well populated as Rochester but Canterbury had two or three times its numbers. It reached a maximum size early in the 14th century after which its population declined, and like the rest of southern England in the middle of that century, it suffered the decimation of its population by the Black Death. Based upon the numbers of inhabitants paying the poll tax, it has been calculated that the population towards the end of the 14th century may have been of the order of 1,700 accommodated in possibly 300 houses, the great majority located in the complex of streets leading off the High Street. It remained the case that comparatively few families resided in the West Borough, and not for another

11　Wat Tyler, by an unknown 19th-century artist (PCF KTMM 33 022).

12 *Old College Gate Tower, one of the remaining parts of Archbishop Courtenay's College of 1348. The tower contains a large baking oven, possibly for baking bread to be given as alms to the poor.*

hundred years or more was the population of the town to increase significantly. There is a reference to a school in Maidstone in 1348 but no other details are known, and it is likely to have been situated near the parish church.

The so-called Peasants' Revolt of 1381 is now recognised as an urban as much as a countryside revolt. Rebel bands numbering thousands, from Essex and north Kent, attacked Canterbury and Rochester and moved on to Maidstone. They beheaded John Southalle, a well-known citizen, and looted his house, as well as William Topclyffe's manor house at the Mote. Whilst the rebels were in Maidstone, Wat Tyler was chosen as their leader. It has been claimed

that he was a Kentishman, and a 16th-century chronicler contended he came from Maidstone. His principal lieutenant, Jack Straw, is said to have been born in Offham, some five miles away. There is no firm evidence to support either claim but it is just possible that if, indeed, both were local men, they may have known one another prior to the revolt.

One of Tyler's close associates was John Ball, a dissident priest being held in the Archbishop's gaol in the town, from which he and the other occupants were released by the rebels a few days after they had released the prisoners from the King's gaol. Ball was a well-known rebel against ecclesiastical authority who had earlier

13 *The remains of the College with the Master's House, now the Music Centre. John Newman suggests this must have been built earlier than the rest because of the rougher masonry and the pairs of ogee-headed lights low in the east wall.*

14 *View of the old College from the river. The Master's Tower is really a gateway and must have been the main entrance to the college from the river.*

15   *All Saints' Church.*

been excommunicated. This was his third incarceration by the ecclesiastical authorities, having been sentenced to imprisonment for life by the Archbishop. He preached a social equality which he claimed that Christ had urged upon his followers, his text being, 'When Adam delved and Eve span / Who was then the gentleman?'

Once the rebels reached London the rising quickly came to an end, with Tyler being killed and Ball hung, drawn and quartered at St Albans. The revolt effectively ended on 15 June but rumbled on in Maidstone. At the end of June, John Gybonn of Maidstone and others were seeking to persuade the Canterbury bailiffs to levy a tax to finance resistance against royal officials in the county. In September, a large group of men from Maidstone and neighbouring villages gathered on Boughton Heath with a view to regaining concessions which the King had made when he met Tyler and his men in London but subsequently revoked. It was

a local attempt to rekindle rebellion which came to nought. Several Maidstone men – John Webbe, Richard Barbour and John Hosyere among them – were brought before the courts for their part in the Peasants' Revolt, but although numbers of prisoners were sentenced to be executed the sentences seem not to have been carried out.

The method of electing the portreeve did not always work smoothly and in 1385 the two nominees, Bartholomew Carewey and Simon Poslynge, both refused to accept the office for reasons which are unknown. As a result their goods were distrained but after almost two months they capitulated and Carewey accepted appointment to the office.

'Le Newark' seems not to have been used to its full extent, for one hundred years after its creation there were only five residents, including retired servants of the Archbishop, and towards the end of the 14th century Archbishop Courtenay

16   *View of All Saints' Church, Archbishop's Palace and College, pre-1880.*

obtained permission from Pope Boniface IX to use the hospital's income, together with that of the parish church, to demolish St Mary's and found a secular college comprising 24 priests who were free to go around the countryside preaching the gospel. A church was to be part of the complex, and work on this began in 1396 when the King authorised the conscription of 48 local masons and labourers for the purpose. By 1398 the construction of All Saints' was completed.

Two

From Religious to Secular Governance, 1400-1600

As well as its use as a building material, ragstone was also of use in time of war when it was fashioned into gunstones for siege engines. In 1419 Henry V ordered 2,000 stone cannon balls from Maidstone whilst, in 1434, 1,214 balls were despatched to the Tower of London.

The Guild of Corpus Christi came into existence in about 1422, its meetings being held in the hall at the bottom of East Street given for that purpose by John Hyssenden. The Guild was a quasi-religious organisation but it also had a social purpose and its membership included many of the important townsfolk. Numbers fluctuated but at times there were as many as 136 brothers and 15 sisters. Some paid nominal amounts for their membership, but the Prior of Leeds and the Abbot of Boxley each paid 3s. 4d. a year, the Master of All Saints' paid 4s., and Sir Henry Ferrers, who was several times High Sheriff of Kent, paid 6s. 8d. The Guild was in receipt of numbers of bequests but the names of the principal donors remain unknown.

The Guild established a chantry at the east end of the north aisle of All Saints' church, where prayers were offered up daily for the souls of departed members. A priest, William Downe, received an annual stipend of £6 13s. 4d., together with a house and garden. As well as providing a meeting place for important citizens, the Guild acted as a charity and maintained several small almshouses for the sick, infirm and poor. There were three in Pudding Lane and six on the south side of the bridge across the Medway. Each dwelling had a ground floor room and a garret. The principal social event for members and their guests was the sumptuous feast held each year on Corpus Christi Day. The fare for one such feast consisted of 128 geese, 52 chickens, 43 pairs of pigeons, 12 pigs, 10 gallons of mild, three quarts of honey, and large quantities of oats, bread, butter, fish, malt, cream, eggs, garlic and spices. Drink consisted of a hogshead [about 50 gallons] of wine and some 45 gallons of ale. Its income enabled the Guild to make purchases of land and houses, and by 1475 it owned nine houses in the town and had six landownings. All of these were let, and brought in an annual rental of 229s. 2d.

The former rectory, now called the Archbishop's Palace, was sufficiently grand by

17 *Corpus Christi Hall in Earl Street is much restored, but the original Hall of the Fraternity lies behind the east end.*

1438 that Henry VI could stay there. By this time the Archbishop no longer needed to appoint his men as executioners on Penenden Heath since a hangman was employed and paid at the rate of 14s. 6d. a year.

In 1450 Maidstone was again involved in rebellion, on this occasion led by Jack Cade, an Irishman who had returned from refuge in France with the intention of conducting an armed struggle against the House of Lancaster. The rebellion commenced from a Kentish base and among local men joining its ranks were William Beale, John Fisher (carpenter), Robert Est, Richard Dyne, Richard Manney (mason), John Baker and John Aston (yeomen), John Mason (wax-chandler), Richard Sabin, John Colney, Stephen Colvey (goldsmith), William Finch (tailor), Robert Shaile, Richard Wood, Thomas Ellis Sen. and his son Thomas Jun. (husbandmen), and Thomas Carter (draper). Est had been one of the first trustees of the Guild of Corpus Christi but was unpopular in the town because of his role as rent collector for the Archbishop of Canterbury and keeper of the

Maidstone gaol. The rebels marched on London where they suffered a heavy defeat. Many were content with a promise of pardons but Cade was killed at Heathfield in Sussex. Maidstone was one of the towns which was collectively pardoned, and the pardon was extended to numbers of the town's inhabitants.

Maidstone was central to yet further rebellion in 1483 when the Duke of Buckingham, a cousin of the Earl of Richmond (later Henry VII), sought to rid the country of Richard III and replace him with Henry. The rallying point for the whole of Eastern England, and Maidstone in particular, was focussed on Earl Rivers, whose residence was at the Mote. It was rumoured that 5,000 men from Kent, Surrey and Sussex were gathered together at Penenden Heath. The rebellion was unsuccessful but that was of little long-term consequence since just 18 months later Richard was killed in battle and Henry took his place as King of England.

By the later 15th century administration of the law was being taken seriously by the portreeve and his assistants, and it had become customary to augment the earlier appointments with four ale-tasters, two bedells and four constables. Regulations issued by the portreeve in 1474 indicate that officials were concerned with the good government and reputation of Maidstone since they forbade disorderly gatherings and games, made rules for employment and apprenticeship, enjoined church attendance and set out to control criminals and suspicious characters. Petty civil and criminal cases were dealt with by the portreeve sitting together with some or all of his brethren.

The College which Archbishop Courtenay had founded had acquired much land in and around Maidstone, as well as elsewhere, and had an income of £40 a year. But just as the usage of the hospital which preceded it had declined, so did that of the College. At the time of the Archbishop's visitation in 1511, only the master and six others remained in residence, although why the numbers should have declined in this way is unclear.

Following the Reformation, the Archbishop was required in 1537 to give his manor of Maidstone to the Crown, together with his residence in the town, the archiepiscopal gaol (which later became the Corporation gaol) and the advowson of All Saints'. The Church in Maidstone, as elsewhere, fared badly from Henry VIII's break with Rome, subsequent suppression of the monasteries, colleges, free chapels and chantries, and the enforcement of Protestantism. All Saints' ceased to be collegiate

18   Earls Place, c.1900. The mansion and grounds were opposite Broughton's house and were the home of the Stafford and Lee families. Richard Lee was Archbishop of York from 1531-44.

19   Ship Inn, *Gabriels Hill.*

and the church's silver and gilt plate, together with other items of value, was sold for £200. The Guild of Corpus Christi was dissolved, and the money raised by the sale of church goods was used to purchase the lands and the Guild Hall of the Fraternity, together with St Faith's chapel and burial ground, and vest them in the town. The Guild Hall was converted into a boys' grammar school. Richard Lee of Earls Place was Archbishop of York from 1531 to 1544.

A description of Maidstone is provided by John Leland, who visited the town in 1538:

> There is in the town a fair College of priests. Courtenay was the founder of the College, where the Master is a Prebendary; the residue are ministers to sing divine service. The Castle [probably the Archbishop's Palace] stands about the middle of the town, being well maintained by the Archbishop of Canterbury. There is a common gaol, or prison of Kent, as in the shire town. Maidstone is a market town, of one long street, well built, and full of inns.

Leland's 'one long street' may have been what is now Week Street, Gabriels Hill and Stone Street. The traveller would have seen numbers of inns around the top end of the High Street for there were at this time the *Ship*, the *George*, the *Bell*, the *Chequers* and the *Bull* in Gabriels Hill. Nearby, in the High Street, were the *Star*, the *Queen's Arms* and the *Swan*.

The portreeve system came to an end when Edward VI granted the town a charter in 1548 which provided for a mayor, jurats and commonalty. The first mayor is named as Richard Heeley. The mayor became clerk of a

20   *The Bell in Gabriels Hill.*

21   Star Inn,
High Street.

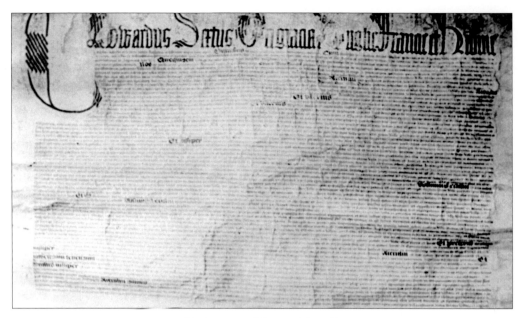

22   *The beginning of the 1549 Town Charter.*

weekly market and the right to hold four fairs annually was also confirmed; Maidstone had developed into an *entrepot*, a trading centre and port at a geographically convenient location. The charter described it as 'the chief port of the river Medway'.

The state of roads in the 15th and 16th centuries was such that heavy goods could not be transported along them in winter, and they were in poor condition for much of the rest of the year too. The King's Gunfounder had his iron works situated on the Horsmonden/Brenchley border and cannon would be taken from there, when road conditions permitted, to Yalding on the Medway, and from there to a depot at Millhall, just outside Maidstone. From thence they would be transported to Chatham Dockyard or the Tower of London by Maidstone vessels.

23   *The old Town Bridge over the Medway, showing boats engaged in industry and commerce.*

In the mid-16th century the town had four hoys of between 30 and 50 tons as well as a number of barges plying the river. There were four wharves on the riverside, the one at the bottom of St Faith's Street being known as the 'Towne Wharf'. Regular cargoes included timber from the Weald destined principally for Chatham Dockyard, and broadcloth, latterly kerseys, for London and intermediate destinations. Return cargoes from London included rags for the papermaking industry growing up in the area, and manure for agriculture. Quantities of wool and dyestuffs from London would be shipped to Rochester, from whence they would go on to Maidstone for both local and much wider distribution throughout the Weald.

24 *A timber wharf close by the new bridge.*

Dissent from the state-ordained religious doctrine had been a feature of Maidstone since the 15th century, when there had been Lollards present in the town. In 1522 an unnamed priest tore down a denunciation of Luther which had been posted at Boxley Abbey, then proceeded to distribute Lutheran tracts in Maidstone High Street. In 1530 Thomas Hilton, a Maidstone curate, was burned at the stake for having carried Lutheran books between the continent and England. Following Mary's accession to the English throne, there came a royal command that all should embrace the Roman Catholic faith, those continuing to adhere to Protestantism being liable to find themselves incarcerated in the town gaol, or worse. On 16 June 1557 two Maidstone men and five women, one of them a sightless girl known as Blind Bess, were burned at the stake in the Fair Meadow because of their refusal to adopt the Catholic faith.

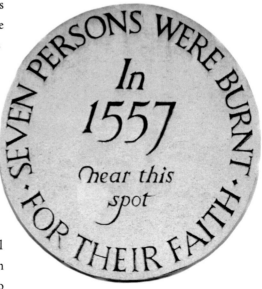

SEVEN PERSONS WERE BURNT · FOR THEIR FAITH · In 1557 near this spot

25 *Commemorative plaque on Waterside.*

In the 1550s an Anabaptist group had its meeting place at a house in Maidstone. One of their number, Thomas Cole a schoolmaster, recanted, but others continued to propagate their faith and at least three of the group, Nicholas Sheterden, Humphrey Middleton and George Brodbridge, were burned at Canterbury in 1555. Dunstan Chittenden died from starvation in Canterbury gaol. It is not known whether the other members of the group, Henry Hart, John Ledley, John Denley (gentleman) and John Newton (pewterer), were able to escape a similar fate, but all the dissenters were either killed or silenced by the Marian persecution and there is no record of Anabaptists in Maidstone for half a century thereafter.

The betrothal of Mary to Archduke Philip of Spain raised fears that the worst features of Catholicism, such as the Inquisition, might be introduced into England. Several Kentish noblemen conspired in an attempt to prevent the marriage, as did their counterparts in other parts of the country. Sir Thomas Wyatt of Allington was designated to lead the rebellion from Kent and it was resolved to commence the challenge from Maidstone on 25 January 1554. Wyatt was accompanied to the High Street by William Tilden, a draper and jurat who rented several fulling mills, and George Maplesden, both of Maidstone, as well as other gentlemen. There he read a proclamation which had been sent to the House of Commons denouncing the projected marriage and urged the townspeople to join in the rebellion. The Sheriff of Kent made no attempt to disperse the force which was gathering since he judged that the inhabitants of Maidstone were in favour of the rising.

On the following day Wyatt and some fifteen hundred men marched on Rochester and hostilities were begun, although much of the fighting with royalist supporters took place not in Kent but in London. Wyatt and his supporters were defeated and surrendered to the royalist forces, and the Sheriff of Kent made many subsequent arrests, including numbers of Maidstone men, among them William Green and William Smythe who were to become mayors of Maidstone in 1560 and 1564 respectively. In all some 78 citizens of Maidstone were indicted, a greater number than came from anywhere else. Those from London numbered only 76, with 37 from Southwark and 30 from Dartford, while those from other towns and villages were mostly numbered in single figures. The indictment of Wyatt was long drawn out and he was not executed until much later. The Sheriff committed the poorer prisoners to Maidstone gaol whilst some others were hanged.

As punishment for joining in the rebellion the Privy Council revoked the town's charter, and Maidstone remained disenfranchised for a period of five years. A new charter containing a number of changes was granted by Elizabeth I in 1559, and for the first time the town was given the right to elect two Members of Parliament; in 1562 Nicholas Barham, who resided at Chillington House, and Henry Fisher were elected, both having previously held the combined offices of recorder and town clerk. The first mayor

26 *Digons, Knightrider Street, was home to several old Maidstone families including the Maplesdens (who forfeited it for their part in the Wyatt rebellion), the Barhams (who provided one of the first two Maidstone Members of Parliament) and the Washingtons (who provided a Maidstone Member of Parliament from 1603 to 1614).*

to be appointed was William Green, and at least three of the 12 jurats – Clement Lutwick, William Tilden and William Smythe – had participated in the Wyatt revolt. The jurisdiction of the Corporation over the River Medway was extended by the charter to include the stretch from East Farleigh to Burham, and it also became entitled to all unmarked swans found within its boundaries. The bridge and river bank maintenance was to be financed by tolls paid at markets and fairs, and the town's right to hold four fairs a year was re-affirmed. For the first time in the town there was complete secular control – that of the corporation and the magistrates – in place of ecclesiastical control.

In 1567 there was an influx of refugees into the south-east from the Low Countries, and the mayor and jurats of Maidstone petitioned the Crown to allow a number of the aliens to settle and establish cloth-working in the town. To this request the royal assent was given. In 1573 Elizabeth showed further concern for the town of Maidstone, and for the desirability of strengthening its industrial base, when she wrote:

> To all our Justices, Officers, Ministers, and Subjects, greeting. Know ye that, for divers special considerations us moving, as well for the help, repair, and amendment of our town of Maidstone, in our county of Kent, by planting in the same men of knowledge in sundry handicrafts, as also for the relief and convenient placing of certain Dutch men, aliens, now residing within our city of London, and elsewhere within our realm of England, being very skilful in divers occupations, arts, handicrafts and faculties, we may lend to the commodity of our realm, and, namely, for the relief of our said town of Maidstone.

This cannot refer to those who had come six years earlier, but to additional numbers of aliens. By 1585 there were 120 adult Walloons

27   *St Faith's Church, Station Road, 1884, built on the site of an earlier church.*

workers: it is recorded that 'the said trade has almost ceased to be carried on by strangers', having been 'learned and taken from them by the kinges borne subjects inhabitinge within the said Towne'. Commercial hop growing began in and around Maidstone in the 16th century but did not become an important element in the economy of the town until the first half of the next.

As the High Street became more and more cluttered in the latter part of the 16th century, the town's fairs, other than the Candlemas Fair, were moved to the Fair Meadow, although the markets remained at the top end of the High Street. The pattern of trade was changing. Broadcloths had been the major item for sale, but by the end of the 16th century there was a requirement that Kentish broadcloth should be sold only at Blackwell Hall in London, so the local sale of cloth to London dealers ceased almost entirely, save for the cheap kersey cloth. Grain from Kent remained an important commodity, with large quantities sold and shipped from Maidstone to London. The sale of fruit and hops in the market for delivery to London was starting to be important to the town at this time.

Almost all important county towns had trade guilds which operated in a religious context prior to the Reformation. Membership of the guild was one way in which a tradesman could become a freeman of the town, an essential for those wishing to set up in business, and by 1551 Maidstone had guilds for artificers, victuallers, drapers, cordwainers and mercers. After 1540 they were concerned not with religion but with economic and, to a lesser extent, political regulation. Together with the magistrates they controlled craft apprenticeships, standards

residing in the town. They were allowed to worship at St Faith's chapel and to use the burial ground there.

Numbers of local residents were employed in the home industry of spinning flax, which was then made into thread by skilled alien workers. Maidstone rapidly acquired almost a monopoly in thread manufacture, which eventually employed some hundreds of individuals. Some forty years after the arrival of the first Walloons the trade had been largely taken over by indigenous of workmanship, and competition between tradesmen. The guilds effectively became part of the Maidstone town oligarchy and the guild wardens were deployed to patrol the town, suppress disorder and eject those whose presence was deemed undesirable; the management of fairs was delegated to them.

Population figures for the 16th century are uncertain. They are unlikely to have exceeded 2,100 at any time, a figure which derives from Archdeacon Harpsfield's visitation of 1557 and is perhaps no greater than the number for the 14th century. With influenza and plague epidemics, the figure may have fallen to between 1,400 and 1,700 by 1563, but towards the end of the century it almost certainly increased. There were several doctors in residence in Maidstone, one of whom, Thomas Vicary, was Sergeant of the King's Surgeons in the reign of Henry VIII. The West Kent Quarter Sessions and the Assizes were held in the town, the Court House being on the site of the present Town Hall. Because the courts were held here, numbers of attorneys and barristers resided in the town, and they appear to have done exceptionally well. When a forced loan was levied in Maidstone and Canterbury at the end of the century about half of those required to pay the highest rate were lawyers. Towards the end of the 16th century there were six licensed teachers in the town, primary schools teaching little more than basic literacy to boys. There is one known instance, in 1585, of an educational facility where girls were taught to sew, read, and make buttons, doubtless by unlicensed teachers.

The poor of the town were numerous and living conditions were unhealthy, with pigs roaming at large, animals slaughtered in the streets, cesspool sanitation and nothing in the way of drainage. For a very few there was accommodation in the almshouses which the town had taken over from the defunct Guild of Corpus Christi. The dwellers in almshouses were, at a time of plague in 1563, subject to a life-threatening edict of the Corporation which required that they should 'do their best endeavours, diligence, and service for the comfort, help, and succour of the sick'. Those refusing were to be turned out of their accommodation and evermore to forfeit any rights and possessions which they may have had.

By 1583 the House of Correction had become the principal centre in the county for punishing tramps and the criminal poor. The West Kent justices ordered special watches on all the major roads and bridges in the area with the intention of keeping such unwelcome strangers out of the town. In 1591 the mayor and jurats warned those in the almshouses that if they continued to keep pigs in what was generally their only living room they would be fined and the animals sold.

Large numbers of soldiers were mustered at Maidstone in 1588 when 3,000 men from West Kent gathered together at Penenden Heath. Two hundred of them were said to be trained soldiers, a further 100 were well armed but only partly trained, and the remainder were imperfectly armed. They were to form part of the much larger army assembled to defend the country against the Spanish Armada but, in the event, were not needed for this purpose. With the town's population doubled in size for the relatively short period they were here, though, they would have had an impact on Maidstone's inns and alehouses.

28 *The principal water conduit, opposite the* Star Inn, *channelled water from Rocky Hill.*

In his will of 1592 George Langley, a deceased weaver, left a house in East Lane to be sold and the proceeds used to provide work for the poor. John Amye, a merchant, left money to provide hemp, flax and wool with which the poor could work. The fund was also used to teach children to make 'cauls, buttons, button moulds, thread, or the winding thereof, or the like easy arts, whereby they might in a very short space get towards their living, at the least, ten or twelve pence weekly'. In

1596 the magistrates noted that 'the number of poor people inhabiting within this town and parish (by means of the long time of scarcity and dearth as well of all kinds of grain and corn and all kinds of victuals) is now grown and come to be very great'. Under Elizabethan legislation there were powers to raise a poor rate locally to assist the indigent, but expenditure from the rate amounted to less than £10 in the 1580s, and the combined efforts of the town and charities in the 15th and 16th centuries were inadequate to meet the widespread problem of poverty. The one respect in which the town was fortunate was in having a healthy supply of water. There was an excellent spring at Rockyhill and water from it was conveyed in pipes across the Medway to conduits in the High Street, the principal conduit being situated opposite the *Star Inn*.

Leland had described the town as 'full of inns', and so it was, not to mention the considerable number of alehouses. There was bear baiting at what was called the Bear Ringle, in the High Street at the top of Mill Lane, and a maypole in the Fair Meadow was the scene of occasional pageants and somewhere the townsfolk would engage in archery practice and other pastimes. There was not yet a theatre in Maidstone, but actors would occasionally perform in the open air, at the grammar school or at the *Star Inn*. The account books show that in most years of the 16th century one or other of the many companies of players which toured the countryside performed in the town. One of the highest payments was the 20s. given in 1586 'to the Queen's players, and in wine bestowed by appointment of Mr Mayor'.

THREE

The Seventeenth-Century Town and the Battle of Maidstone

In 1601 there was much resentment shown against the authorities in Maidstone and the magistrates introduced swingeing penalties for those who used 'ill, lewd or scoffing speech towards the mayor or any of the jurats'. Poverty and plague were widespread and in the plague year of 1604-5 the proceeds of the poor rate reached a level of £46. This was four and a half times what it had been some 25 years previously and was possibly one of the reasons for the ill feeling. By the early 17th century the Corporation was better able to deal with law and order, once a matter for the trade guilds which were now in a state of decline. The Corporation re-established them in 1605 but they played no part in the town's affairs after they were dissolved by the Burghmote in 1613. An Upper Court House, with a court of 'Nisi Prius' (a direction that a case should be heard by a single judge and jury), was installed

about 1608 near the Court House in the High Street, now renamed the Lower Court House. The Assize judges sat in the new court to deal with civil cases and in the old court for criminal cases. The Quarter Sessions for West Kent were held in the Lower Court House.

Pargetting became fashionable as an adornment of the façade of buildings in the 17th century, and what remains of one of the

29 *Court Houses and Market Place, High Street, 1623.*

25

30 Bank Street. This Jacobean house was originally fully pargetted but much was removed in the early 1800s (above left).

31 Pargetted house, Week Street (above).

32 Seventeenth-century pargetted house in Bank Street (lower section of building) (left).

33   *Astley House, with pargetting. The High Street residence of the Bliss family, now demolished.*

earliest examples in Maidstone, dated 1611, are the Royal Arms and the Prince of Wales feathers on a building in Bank Street. A later example, dated 1680, is in Week Street. The decoration of both buildings would have been far more extensive in its original state.

Until 1608 the corn market was held in the space under what became the Upper Court House and corn was stored in the room above. A meat market was held each Thursday at the Market Cross at the top of the High Street, a shambles being situated between the Market Cross and the county gaol. In 1612 the Corporation ordered that butchers should not trade during the hours of services on Sundays but only before eight o'clock in the morning and after the evening service. Country butchers complained in 1629

that the market was held so late that, travelling home at night in the winter, they ran the risk of being robbed, and the Corporation agreed the market should end at 4 p.m. in winter.

The growing needs of the town's inhabitants made it imperative that water resources, which had remained essentially unchanged for over one hundred years, should be augmented, and in response to a 1625 memorial from residents the Corporation erected a further conduit at the lower end of the High Street.

In the 1620s and 1630s there existed in Maidstone a separatist group which was a matter of much concern to Archbishop Laud, a High Churchman particularly opposed to any form of dissent. These radical Protestants saw Christianity as a personal faith rather than

34 The Old Market Cross, Maidstone, *by William Jeffreys* (*18th century*) (PCF KTMM 10 024).

read a prayer against Scottish religious practices and ignoring the King's request to read the Book of Sports for the Lord's Day. In 1641 his suspension was lifted at the request of Sir Edward Deering, the doyen of a leading Kentish family. At the time of Wilson's arrival, Maidstone parish was described by Robert Swinnock, a jurat, as 'formerly a very profane town inasmuch as I have seen Morris dancing, cudgel playing, stool-ball, crickets and many other sports openly and publickly on the Lord's Day'. These practices had largely ceased before Wilson

one of public ceremony and regarded the 1559 Prayer Book, with its emphasis on ceremonials and vestments, as popish. In 1635 Laud issued an edict that the Dutch, who had been allowed to practise their Calvinist religion at St Faith's chapel, should give up their faith and practise that of the established church at All Saints'. He reported to Charles I that there were 'very many refractory persons to the government of the Church of England about Maidstone', but his instruction had effect for only a short period as St Faith's was soon opened again and for a long period afterwards was used as a chapel by nonconformists.

In 1643 the Rev. Thomas Wilson, a Puritan, was appointed as rector of All Saints'. He had previously been at Otford where he had persuaded the fulling mills to cease work on Sundays. He had also been in trouble with the ecclesiastical authorities and was suspended for refusing to

arrived but he went even further and, among other things, urged the townspeople to 'forbear vain walking [and] idling at their doors', and adjured them not to draw water on Sundays but to do it on Saturday nights. The result was that the streets were largely empty after the Sunday sermon. Wilson was so successful in keeping the Lord's Day sacred that a judge at the Assizes in Maidstone was moved to say that 'in all his Circuit he never came to a town where the Lord's Day was so strictly observed'. The conflict between King and Commons at this time continued to arouse strong feelings in the town and in 1647 Wilson's house was attacked by conservative elements.

By the middle of the 17th century the population of the town had grown to around three thousand. In Kent, Rochester and Dover were of an equal size and only Canterbury had more people. The number of houses is known only approximately and there were some 110 in the High Street, 60 in Week Street, 25 on Gabriels Hill and 100 in Stone Street, with 44 in the West Borough. The supply of fresh water to the town had been augmented only 20 years earlier, but by 1645 it was once again found to be inadequate. An additional conduit, towards the upper end of the High Street, was connected to the supply from the spring at Rockyhill.

In 1648 a battle was fought in the centre of Maidstone. Maidstone played little or no direct part in the early years of the Civil Wars, although numbers of those opposed to taking an oath of loyalty to the Parliament were local residents. Among those actively involved were members of the Covert family, who fought on the King's side, and Sir Jacob Astley, who resided at the Archbishop's Palace and was a member of the

King's Council of War. The rupture between Charles I and Parliament had reached a climax in 1642 and Parliamentary armed forces were sent to Kent to ensure there were no disturbances in a fractious county already at odds with the County Committee, a creature of Parliament. Maidstone tradesmen anticipated trouble from the soldiers and closed their shops, but in the event there were no disturbances.

The immediate cause of the Kentish Rising of 1648 was a petition to Parliament urging the end of the war, effectively on Royalist terms. It was signed by, among others, Lambard Godfrey, a future Recorder of Maidstone. The contents of the petition angered Parliament and, no reconciliation proving possible, the County Committee based at Maidstone ordered those who were trained soldiers to muster on Penenden

35   *Great Buckland, 17th-century home of the Earl of Aylesford, was demolished in 1873.*

36 *Sir William Brockman 1642, Colonel in Chief of Royalist forces at the Battle of Maidstone, by Cornelis Jansenns van Ceulen (PCF KTMM 037 023).*

Heath with a view to preventing any tumultuous meetings in the county. But no more than 20 Maidstone men presented themselves for service in the Parliamentary cause.

Parliament then decided that General Sir Thomas Fairfax, commander of the Parliamentary forces, should bring the county of Kent to heel. He set out on 1 June 1648, at the head of perhaps as many as 4,000 troops, to engage what may have been 3,000 armed Royalist supporters situated in Maidstone and a large number of others stationed between Aylesford and Rochester. As part of the Maidstone defences against Fairfax's forces, Stone Street had been barricaded with trees, and a stockade was raised across Gabriels Hill with an earthwork at the top. Cannons covered each of the four streets at its intersection with the High Street, and Royalists were installed in almost every house. Before the conflict began some 800 Royalist reinforcements arrived in Maidstone

from elsewhere but, unlike the Parliamentary forces, the Royalists were not for the most part trained soldiers.

After five hours of fierce fighting many Royalists had fled from the field, those who remained being driven into the churchyard of St Faith's where they were left with no option but to surrender. Their leaders were killed or captured and 1,300 of the rank and file taken prisoner. The Parliamentarians captured 500 horses, 3,000 arms and eight cannon, but around eighty of their own soldiers were killed in the fighting. Many of the killed or captured Royalists were not residents of Maidstone, coming from other parts of Kent and from London, but a considerable number of the 300 who were killed were local men. The Maidstone church registers of marriages over the next six or seven years provide evidence for this. In 1655 widows were represented in 40 per cent of the more than 100 marriages which took place in that year, but there is no record in either the borough or church records for 1648 that the battle took place at all. Nor are burials recorded in the parish registers for the three days following the battle.

37 *Andrew Broughton's house in Earl Street.*

In December 1648 plans were being laid for the trial of Charles I, the army having removed from Parliament those Members who they thought might side with the King. The six Kentish Members ejected included Sir Humphrey Tufton and Thomas Twisden, the Maidstone MPs. Maidstone men who were on the side of Parliament included Andrew Broughton, a lawyer who was Mayor of Maidstone and one of the town's representatives in the Rump of the Long Parliament until 1653. He was appointed as Clerk to the Court of Parliament which tried the King and at the end of the trial he read the sentence of death. Thomas Trapham, a Maidstone surgeon, carried out the embalming of the body after Charles's execution.

During the period between 1649 and the Restoration in 1660, the Protectorate did not command widespread support in Maidstone. Thomas Kelsey, the major-general who was the government's representative in Kent, was particularly concerned about the attitude prevailing in the town at the time of the 1656 parliamentary elections. He wrote to Cromwell that Royalists and Presbyterians in Maidstone were combining 'against you and the government, and the spirit is generally bitter against swordsmen, decimators [those charged with levying a 10 per cent tax on the estates of known Royalist supporters] and others'.

In the middle of the century two Quakers, John Stubbs and William Caton, were put in the stocks in the town and 'cruelly whipped with cords in a bloody manner'. Nineteen others of their faith were incarcerated in Maidstone gaol in 1663 for refusing to take an oath of allegiance. Joseph Wright had been appointed as the first Baptist pastor in the town, and as a dissenter he was imprisoned in Maidstone gaol on one pretext or another for some twenty years. He was eventually released when James II was on the throne and making efforts to conciliate nonconformists, and he ordered the mayor and jurats of Maidstone to confer on Wright the office of chief magistrate without requiring him to take an oath of allegiance to King and government. Wright was mayor for almost a year, whilst he continued as pastor to his flock. When he died his body was interred in the burial ground south of Tovil which Simon Pine had gifted to the Baptists.

Broadcloth was still being produced in the first half of the century but as the trade struggled to compete with producers in other parts of the country and in mainland Europe, weavers turned to a narrower manufacturing base, producing a checked fabric and serge and cloth for gowns, although even this work ceased towards the end of the century. The production of linen thread expanded and Maidstone's near-monopoly in England continued. It has been suggested that up to two thousand local people were, directly and indirectly, engaged in thread making.

Brewing of ale had been a cottage industry in Maidstone for a long time, but in around 1650 brewing of bitter beer on a commercial basis, using hops, was introduced by John Saunders at the Lower Brewery in Lower Stone Street. At much the same time the Upper Brewery was operating in what is now Brewer Street. A third brewery, situated near St Faith's Green, was purchased by John Cripps of the Upper Brewery in 1668.

Maidstone was at this time a relatively small-scale producer of saltpetre, a component of gunpowder, as well as of gunpowder itself, and

38   *St Faith's Green in 1860.*

on the outskirts of the town on the river Len were several paper mills. Not only was the local water eminently suitable for papermaking but the Maidstone barges travelling to London returned with rags to be converted into paper. Ravenscroft in the 17th century was the first glassmaker to make high quality flint glass, for which purpose it obtained white sand from Maidstone.

The poor were numerous in Maidstone and the Hearth Tax records of 1664 give some idea of the level of poverty in the town. The poorest people were exempt from paying the tax and in Maidstone these amounted to one half of all households, compared with a figure of less than one third for the county as a whole. Epidemics were no respecters of rich or poor, but because of their squalid living conditions the poor were most exposed to the plague which was rife in the town and resulted in many deaths in the first three decades of the century, and again in 1665-6.

The magistrates were required to set a daily wage for labourers and, sitting at Maidstone in 1669, they decided that in summer it should be 14d., or 7d. with meat, whilst more should be paid at harvest time. In winter the rates were set at 10d., or 5d. with meat. These amounts were to remain unchanged until 1722. A small amount of assistance was given to those in the town in the greatest need. Among 17th-century benefactors, Sir Henry Cutt of Thurnham willed £3 a year for the relief of the poor, and in 1618 the Rev. Robert Gunsley, of Titsey in Surrey, left the rents of the rectory of Broadhampton in Devonshire to be used to provide bread and clothing for the poor of Maidstone and Rochester. Bequests were commonly for the disbursement of small amounts of money, bread, fuel or clothing. The parish officers were enabled to alleviate poverty to a small extent from money raised by the poor rate, which in the 1660s amounted to £450. But not all those in need were able to benefit, and there was a 'cage' by the gaol in the High Street in which beggars and vagabonds who had arrived from elsewhere were locked up; they received little in the way of relief.

The 'cage' was moved in 1654 from the Lower Court House to east of the Medway bridge.

At the Restoration in May 1660, or perhaps a month or so earlier, Broughton foresaw that he would be tried for regicide if he remained in the country. Without any notice to the Corporation of the town of which he was still the mayor, he fled to Geneva, where he was to spend the rest of his life. In 1661, with Charles II on the throne, members of Corporations were required to swear an oath of allegiance to the monarch and the government and those who would not were removed from office. In Maidstone six jurats and 16 common councillors suffered this fate.

The river trade to the Medway towns and to London assumed greater importance during the 17th century, with increased volumes arising from the expanded populations of the capital and, to a lesser extent, of Rochester and its surroundings. Improvements were made to the river and its banks between 1661 and 1668, important changes being the construction of a towpath, which allowed the use of horses, the deepening of the river and the erection of locks.

Samuel Pepys records in his *Diary* that he visited Maidstone in 1669: 'In the street I did also buy and send to our inne, the Bell, a dish of fresh fish. And so having walked all round the town and found it very pretty as most towns I ever saw, though not very big, and people of good fashion in it, we to our inne and had a good dinner.' In 1671 Walter Fisher bequeathed property from which the rents were to enable three poor boys, the sons of freemen, to be taught a trade, whilst every year £2 was to be paid to indigent widows of the town.

Thomas Bliss was managing the brewery near St Faith's Green by 1678, although the Cripps family maintained a financial interest in the business. By 1682 the Lower Brewery had changed hands several times and was owned by Bliss, who had also acquired several of the town's hostelries. By far the most important development in agriculture by the end of the century had become the trade in hops. Travelling from Maidstone to Rochester in 1682, Celia Fiennes 'came by a great many fine hopp-yards where they were at work pulling the hopps'. The town charter had given the authority to hold an annual hop fair in the same year and Fiennes, who presumably visited in the late summer, recorded her impressions of the town and the market:

> Maidstone town is a very neate market town as you shall see in the Country, its buildings are mostly of timber worke the streets are large the Market Cross runs down in the middle of the greate street a good way, there being three divisions in it one good Cross for fruite another for corne and another for all sorts of things, 2 of which is built over for the Town Hall and public use; there is also a large Gaol; this streete, notwithstanding the hall and cross stands in the midst, is yet a good breadth on each side and when it comes to meete in one is very broad and runs down a great length, quite to the bridge cross the Medway, which is not very broad here yet it beares Barges that bring up burdens to the town; it seemes to divide the town for beyond the Bridge are buildings whole streetes which run along the river, there are very pretty houses about the town look like the habitations of rich men, I believe it's a wealthy place, there are several pretty streetes; this was Market day being Thursday and it seemed to be well furnish'd with all sorts of commodityes and I observed there was great quantet'ys of Leather but could not learn what particular thing was their staple Comodity or tradeing in, but in generall it seemed to be like a little faire for the variety of wares tho' they told me that was not so full a Market as some dayes, because the Country people were taken up aboute their hopping so could not bring things to Market.

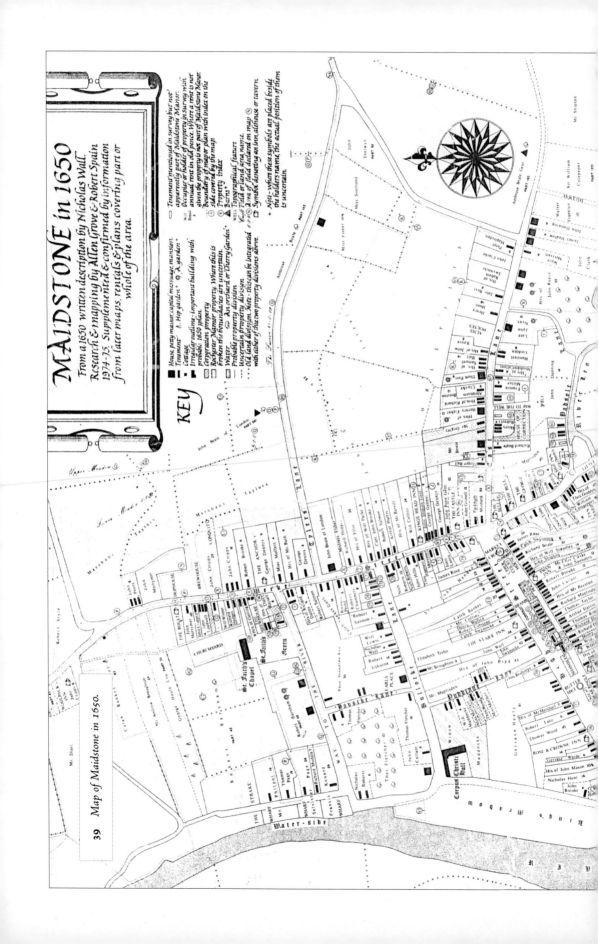

MAIDSTONE in 1650

From a 1650 written description by Nicholas Wall. Research & mapping by Allen Grove & Robert Spain 1974–75. Supplemented & confirmed by information from later maps, rentals & plans covering part or whole of the area.

KEY

House, petty manor capital messuage, mansion. Tenement. A. Hop garden+ ⊙ A garden + cottage.

Irregular outline–important building with probable 1650 plan.

Corporation property.

Rochester Manor property. Where this is broken its boundaries are uncertain.

⊙ Water. ⊙ An orchard or Cherry Garden.

Probable property division.

Uncertain property division.

Old land division. Note- this can be integrated with either of the two property divisions above.

Tenement mentioned in survey but not apparently part of Maidstone Manor. Occupier or holder of property in survey with annual rent in old pence. Where a rent is not given the property is not part of Maidstone Manor.

Boundary of manor plan with index on the side covered by the map.

Ⓟ Property index

▲ Barns

WELL Topographical feature.

Coul Field, or land area name.

Ⓝ Area of field declared on map Ⓝ

☀ Symbol denoting an inn, alehouse or tavern.

• Note– when these symbols are placed beside the holders name, the actual position of them is uncertain.

39   Map of Maidstone in 1650.

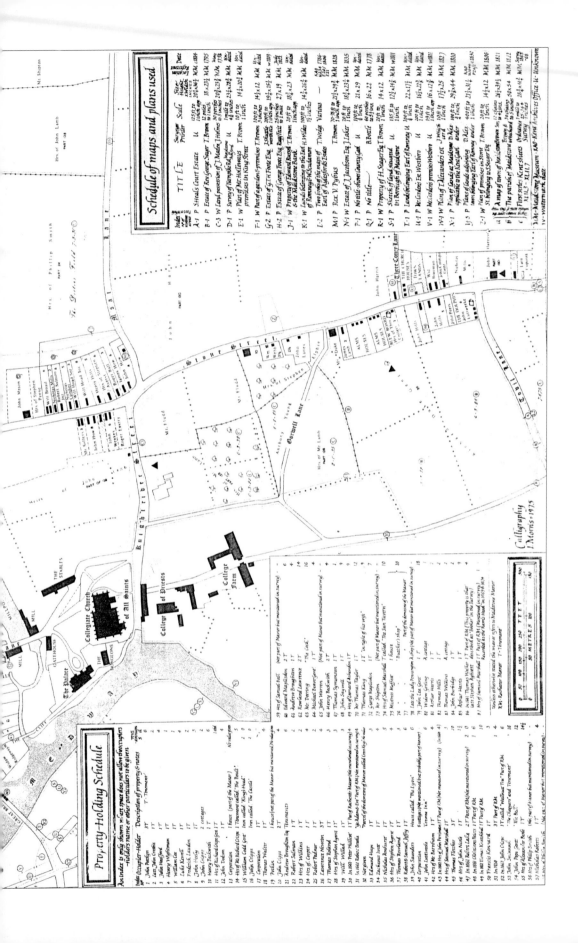

40 *Banks Almshouses, Faith Street, erected in 1699.*

In the second half of the century clover was being grown extensively from seed imported through Maidstone, and by the turn of the next the country was producing clover in such quantities that it was being exported.

In 1696 the poor rate raised the sum of £696, the highest amount since the rate was first introduced, and in 1697 Sir John Banks bequeathed funds sufficient to provide six almshouses for poor parishioners in St Faith's Street. The houses had three small rooms and a little garden and remain to this day. By the end of the 17th century Maidstone had six ships engaged in a regular trade in agricultural produce with London. On their return journeys they brought manufactured goods, wine, tobacco and dairy products to meet the needs of the town and the surrounding area.

FOUR

The Town Charter Forfeited and Developing Industries, 1700-1775

In May 1701 a Kentish Petition urging that the safety and religion of England should be preserved against the powers of France and Spain was drawn up at the Maidstone Quarter Sessions and signed by deputy lieutenants, justices and many freeholders, and then presented to the House of Commons. The petition was couched in moderate terms but was considered by the House to be an impertinence and the five justices who had presented it were imprisoned. Two of them, Thomas Culpepper and Justinian Champneys, were Maidstone men. Parliament had decided the prisoners should be detained until the end of the session but they were released a month early, in June, when it appeared their detention was illegal. On their return there were great celebrations in Maidstone, concluding with a huge bonfire.

When the outcome of the 1701 parliamentary election for the Maidstone constituency was known and Sir Robert Marsham (Whig) and Thomas Bliss (Tory) were returned, Parliament was petitioned to annul the result on the grounds of malfeasance and bribery. Both Whigs and Tories, when in power, would appoint as freemen

those whom they considered would provide them with support, and among these were a number in receipt of poor relief. The parliamentary committee declared that those in receipt of alms or charity did not have the right to vote and so the result was nullified.

In the ensuing by-election of 1702, Bliss, the owner of the Lower Brewery, was accused of bribery by making loans which were understood to be non-returnable and providing free drinks for all at his public houses at election time. Once again the election was declared void and Parliament ordained that no further election was to be allowed in Maidstone during that parliamentary session. Bribery was not uncommon in 18th-century politics. Some Cambridge academics who were touring Kent in 1735 recorded, in respect of Maidstone, that Thomas Hope, a butcher and one of the town's MPs in the 1727 Parliament, had given those butchers who had voted for him silver handles to their steels.

In 1707 Robert Rowland, born in Maidstone but residing in London, left £120 in trust to provide loans to set up in trade 12 young men just out of their apprenticeships. They were each required to pay 6s. 8d. annual interest and £2 of the resulting sum was to be given to the poor of the town. In 1711 the minister of All Saints', Dr Woodward, endowed the Bluecoat School for poor children and this was subsequently sustained by other bequests.

Maidstone's specialist fairs and markets flourished in the 18th century. The principal location for them was the Fair Meadow by this time, although some trade remained in the High Street. There was a cattle and sheep fair, many of the cattle being brought from Wales, but the day-to-day sale of cattle took place in Bullock Lane (Earl Street) and in the High Street. The cloisters of the boys' grammar school served as the venue for the sale of hops.

41 *Head and Shoulders of a Girl Wearing the Bonnet as Worn by Girls of Dr Woodward's School, Maidstone, late 19th century, by Jane Dean (32.1894).*

42 *Market buildings and colonnade.*

Another market specialised in fruit from the Kentish orchards although it was, by then, becoming the practice to purchase fruit directly from the orchard. Sir Edward Filmer of East Sutton kept accounts of the produce of his orchards, which he sold to Maidstone wholesalers: in 1716 he sold 438 bushels of apples and pears to a wholesaler named Oliver for £25, and in 1718, 390 bushels were sold to Humphrey Porter for £25. Fruit had been scarce that year and hence it fetched a better price. In the same year he sold 20 bushels of walnuts (he estimated this to be about 20,000 nuts) to Porter for £3. The usual practice was for the wholesaler to pick the fruit and the grower to pay the tithe and the packing and carriage to Maidstone market. In 1718 Filmer recorded that pickers were paid 9s. a week, which generally worked out at 1s. 6d. for 10 bushels, and packing and carriage to Maidstone cost a further 1s. 6d. Filmer noted, 'Never sell your apples by the lump till after St James's Day, the 25th of July, because they are so small before, that no one can judge of the quantity.'

Fish, vegetables and corn continued to be traded in the High Street, but street markets generally were coming under increasing pressure from shops, as well as taverns and alehouses, which were engaging in the sale of goods. Daniel Defoe, writing in the 1720s, referred approvingly to the town:

[Maidstone] is a considerable town, very populous, and the inhabitants generally wealthy; 'tis the county town, and the river Medway is navigable to it by large hoys of fifty or sixty tons burthen, the tide flowing quite up to the town ... Round this town are the largest cherry orchards and the most of them that are in any part of England ... Here likewise, and in the country adjacent, are great quantities of hops planted, and this is called the Mother of Hop Grounds in England; being the first place in England where hops were planted in any quantity ... From this town, and the neighbouring parts, London is supplied with more particulars than from any single market town in England ... This neighbourhood of persons of figure and quality, makes Maidstone a very agreeable place to live in, and where a man of letters, and of manners, will always find suitable company, both to divert and improve himself; so that here is, what is not often found, namely, a town of very great business and trade, and yet full of gentry, of mirth, and of good company ... There is not much manufacturing in this county; what is left, is chiefly at Canterbury, and in this town of Maidstone, and the neighbourhood.

The poor of the town continued to receive assistance both through the proceeds of the poor rate and the benevolence of some inhabitants. In 1719 Robert Bliss erected a workhouse on land he owned in Knightrider Street, the principal

purpose of which was to earn money from the labours of the inmates and do away with the system of out-relief, which was regarded by many ratepayers as unnecessarily generous. In Maidstone, as elsewhere, these aims were achieved initially, but over the years the workhouse was much less successful. Once it was made available, the parish officers issued a notice to claimants that 'all who come for weekly pay should go hither', and little more than half the poor who had previously received payment now sought any relief. Expenditure on the poor in the two previous years had been £929 and £1,062, but by 1724 the amount was reduced to £530. This was achieved in part by hiring out inmates to farmers and others, and in part by the harsh nature of the workhouse regime which served to discourage claimants. In 1727 Mary Duke provided three houses in East Lane to accommodate poor Presbyterian women, whilst in 1735 Edward Hunter provided for six almshouses on the Mote Road.

Maidstone and Canterbury were the only two Kentish towns to have newspapers at a date earlier than 1830. The *Maidstone Mercury* was published in 1725 and the *Maidstone Journal* in 1737, but both endured for less than one year, perhaps because of the ready availability of London newspapers and the effects of the Stamp Acts, which imposed a heavy burden on all newspapers. Not until 1786 did Maidstone have an ongoing newspaper in the form of the *Maidstone Journal*.

In 1715 the mayor and jurats decided that only they could vote in the election of jurats, and the common councilmen were deemed to be entitled no longer to a voice in the matter. The revised practice remained in force until 1730 when the councilmen commenced an action in the courts with a view to overturning the decision. They were successful on the grounds that the 1649 charter did accord a vote to the councilmen, and as a result the election of most of the jurats was invalidated. By 1740 only six of them remained in office and in a further court action their election too was declared null and void. With no jurats in office, the Corporation was automatically dissolved and the charter thereby forfeited, and for some six years the town was without a mayor or town clerk. Not until June 1747 did the Privy Council grant a new charter, in which Edward Hunter was named as the mayor and which provided for 12 jurats and 40 common councillors. Thus was brought to an end this particular constitutional battle between the different groupings on the Council.

By the 1700s hop growing in Maidstone and the surrounding area had become of great importance to the town both commercially and as a source of employment. In 1697 Celia Fiennes found Maidstone market 'not so full … because the country people were taken up aboute their hopping'. William Marshall wrote that, 'the town of Maidstone is nearly deserted, in the height of the season. Tradesmen's daughters, even of the higher classes; and those of yeomen and farmers of the first rank, and best education, are seen busy at the hop bins.' Hops provided the basis for the commercialisation of brewing, and the industry was to expand very considerably in Maidstone throughout the next two centuries. Another drinks industry in the town involved the distillation of the juice of blackcurrants to produce a fruit liqueur which went by the name of 'gazle wine', 'gazle' being a local word for the blackcurrant.

There were, by the early 1700s, several mills on the Len and Loose rivers which had once been employed in the fulling process but which were now engaged in papermaking. In the early days of papermaking these mills would have employed between six and 15 workers, producing hand-made

43   *Lenworth Mill, Water Lane.*

paper with little assistance from machinery, but some were to develop into large enterprises. James Whatman took over Old Turkey Mill and two other mills in 1739 and his works continued until recent times, producing paper of the highest quality. The Upper Tovil Mill and Bridge Mill were purchased much later by Albert Reed, a papermaker who moved to the Maidstone area from Exeter.

Dymer's itinerant theatre company visited the town in 1730 and returned in 1732, when it erected a booth in the yard of the *Star Inn* and presented performances from there. In 1731 All Saints' church suffered serious damage when the spire was struck by lightning on the night of 2 November. The church was adjacent to the river, where there was an unlimited supply of water, but it was of no avail since the fire began at the top of the 172 ft edifice and burned downwards. The main building was largely undamaged, but the spire has never been replaced.

Some assistance to trade in the 18th century was afforded by further improvements to the Medway navigation. There had throughout the 17th century been pressure to extend the navigable section so that river traffic could proceed more readily from Maidstone, at least as far as Tonbridge, but such improvements had generally been opposed by local interests. Although a Parliamentary Act of 1664 had authorised improvements, nothing was done in practice until 1739, when legislation created the Medway Navigation Company, charged with the duty of effecting improvements and managing the river. The improvements were not extended beyond Tonbridge, although the Act allowed for this, but the river did become navigable by hoys of 50 to 60 tons as far as that town. This proved an advantage for Maidstone traders, particularly those engaged in the grocery trade, for they were now able to supply groceries, much originating

44 *Bridge Mill, Tovil.*

from London, to meet the needs of Tonbridge. Maidstone was also the supply centre for a variety of goods over much of the Weald. Coal from Newcastle and Sunderland arrived at Maidstone by river and was distributed therefrom.

By 1735 the gaol in the High Street was proving to be both an annoyance to inhabitants of the area and inadequate for the numbers sentenced to imprisonment, and in the following year Parliament sanctioned the building of a new prison. The process was delayed by disputes between the justices of the East and West Divisions of the county over whether the West Division should meet the cost alone or whether it should be divided between the two of them, and it was not until 1746 that a new prison was built in East Lane. In 1753 the Lower Court House and the Brambles prison in the High Street were demolished and the Town Hall was built on the site. An upper room of the Town Hall was then designated as the town prison.

45   *The Town Hall was built in 1753.*

46   *Birthplace of William Woollett, Engraver to George III.*

William Woollett was born in East Lane (now King Street) in 1735. His father was a foreman thread-maker and, later, landlord of the *Turk's Head* public house in Rose Yard. William became one of London's leading engravers and was appointed as Engraver to George III. When he died in 1785 he was buried in St Pancras churchyard and there is a memorial to him in Westminster Abbey.

A Presbyterian congregation formed about the time of the Reformation had been allowed the use of St Faith's chapel in 1672. Four of their ministers, George Swinnock, Samuel Borfet, Robet Perrott and John Durrant, had all been expelled from the established church for refusing to accept the Act of Uniformity. The congregation removed to Market Street Chapel when it was erected in 1736, but in 1745 the Minister, Benjamin Mills, left Maidstone and the appointment of his successor led to a split in the congregation. Most had by then become Arians and denied the divinity of Christ, tolerating worship of God the Father only, and they appointed a minister, Israel Lewis, who shared their beliefs. Lewis's successor was William Hazlitt, the father of the more famous critic and essayist, who held office from 1770 to 1780. Other members of the Market Street congregation seceded and founded what was to become the Week Street Independent Congregation, with Herbert Jenkins as their Minister.

The army was divided up into county regiments for the first time in 1759. The West Kent Militia was one of the first to be formed, and from time to time it had an impact on the town of Maidstone. The Militia was embodied with a quota of 960 men and with Earl Romney

of the Mote as its Colonel. The troops served on a part-time basis and were mustered for full-time service only in response to an external military threat to the homeland. Each man served for five years and soldiers assembled in the vicinity of Maidstone in June of each year for 28 days' training. This created problems for the farmers of Maidstone and elsewhere, since it took men away from their work for a long period at what was usually a busy time of the year. The hostelries of the town would be busy with soldiers for one month each year, and whilst this would bring increased revenue to the shops and inns there were social problems associated with being a garrison town.

During the 18th century year-round access to Maidstone became easier. The maintenance and condition of roads was improved once they were turnpiked, since this process centralised responsibility and provided money for their upkeep. The Maidstone to Rochester and Maidstone to Cranbrook roads had been turnpiked by the middle

47 *Portrait of William Hazlitt, by John Hazlitt (1767-1837)* (67.1909.24).

48 *Week Street Congregational Church.*

of the century and the Maidstone to Tonbridge road was turnpiked in 1766, although it then gave rise to local resistance, Maidstone people resenting the tolls on roads which they had previously traversed free of any charge. The Quarter Sessions ordered the Sheriff to remove the tollgate at Penenden Heath, since its erection was deemed to be illegal, but a year later it was found to have been replaced and the Sheriff was again instructed to ensure that it was removed, and was to be removed should it ever be re-erected in the future. The townsfolk sought representation on the turnpike trust committee, and demanded that there should be no tollgate within half a mile of the town or, if there were to be one, that townspeople should be exempt from tolls, but all these requests were ignored by the trustees.

It is possible to get some idea of the occupations of Maidstone folk in the middle of the century from pollbooks, which contain this information in respect of freemen of the town. An analysis of the pollbook for the 1761 election of the two Maidstone Members of Parliament shows that there were 490 freemen resident in the town (there were many others who lived elsewhere) who voted. The 12 most numerous occupations were as follows:

Occupation	Number
Labourer	48
Cordwainer (shoemaker)	38
Waterman (and hoyman)	38
Carpenter	25
Victualler	18
Gent	16
Papermaker	14
Barber	13
Blacksmith	13
Tailor	13
Gardener	11
Farmer	10

The number of labourers is evidence of the fact that both Whigs and Tories would give the freedom to those who supported their politics, regardless of their position in life. The list also included three weavers, six thread twisters and two flax dressers, so the cloth-making and thread-twisting industries continued in a small way well into the 18th century, although they had largely come to an end by that time.

A serious riot occurred at the gaol in August 1765. Led by two prisoners, Pingano, a Genoese, and Benvenuto, a group on the way to divine service stabbed the gaoler with his own broadsword, and rendered the chaplain, John Denne, unconscious. All the prisoners were liberated and the gaol's armoury seized. The prisoners fired on the inhabitants of East Lane, who had assembled, and several were wounded. After three days troops engaged the convicts near Plaxtol and killed several, including the ringleaders. Other rioters were tried and executed.

Smallpox epidemics resulted in 70 deaths in 1753 and almost 100 in 1760. In 1766 Daniel Sutton was employed by the parish to provide inoculation against the disease and the number of deaths in that year fell to fifty-four. By 1772 the parish was prepared to pay for the inoculation of the poor at a cost not exceeding 5s. 3d. per person. Other epidemics, such as cholera and typhus, remained as potential dangers.

In December 1770 the town had an addition to its leisure facilities when the tiny 'New Theatre' opened at the lower end of the High Street near the Fair Meadow and gave three performances weekly for two weeks.

FIVE

Maidstone Journal, *The Revolutionary War and Town Improvements, 1775-1803*

In 1778 some 15,000 troops were in tented accommodation at Coxheath, three miles outside Maidstone. An influx of this nature caused problems for the town of Maidstone and its attendant attractions of inns and alehouses, but perhaps the greater impact was the demand placed by the troops and their horses on local food supplies, a problem which was especially acute during the periods of poor harvests. The troops stationed at Coxheath were reviewed in November by George III who, in response to an address from the Mayor and Corporation of Maidstone, conferred a knighthood on William Bishop, the mayor.

The commercial importance of Maidstone and the growth of its shopping facilities can be judged by the Shop Tax of the 1780s. Maidstone, Canterbury, Greenwich and Chatham were all required to pay more than £75, Woolwich paid £50, Bromley only £22 and Sevenoaks £14. John Denne, the incumbent of All Saints', carried out an enumeration of Maidstone residents in 1782 and found that the parish had a population of 5,755, of which 5,028 were living in the town. Four streets contained more than 100

houses: Stone Street had 192 houses with 891 inhabitants; High Street and Middle Row had 173 houses with 909 inhabitants; Week Street had 136 houses with 675 inhabitants; and East Lane (later King Street) had 117 houses with 676 inhabitants. The last of these was one of the narrowest lanes in the town. Most other streets had between 14 and 35 houses, only Gabriels Hill and Earl Street having as many as 40, while the West Borough had 73 houses with 346 inhabitants. We cannot be certain how accurate Denne's head counting was, though. The 1801 census, a more reliable although still imperfect guide, indicated that the population had risen to 8,027 individuals living in 1,346 houses.

The *Maidstone Journal and Kentish Advertiser* was published weekly from 1786 by John Blake, a printer, bookseller and stationer at the King's Arms Printing Office and the town's mayor in 1799. Like all provincial newspapers of the period, it relied heavily on the London newspapers for news of Parliament, the Court, and the progress of wars, all of which it published extensively, even judged by 21st-century standards. A week after the storming of the Bastille the publisher was

49   *View of the High Street, 1820.*

praising the French Revolution, 'For as England, say the people, is free so will France be'. As the Revolution developed the *Journal* became more critical, and in 1793, with the outbreak of the Revolutionary War, the editor's position was made abundantly clear:

[Over nearly eleven years] he has devoted himself to its publication, during which length of time he has uniformly adhered to one object, the support of the present Government [that of Pitt the Younger] as without a necessary respect to the laws, and a due regard to order and subordination, he is perfectly convinced that *no community* can exist with safety to itself or happiness to the

50   *View of Week Street, c.1800.*

individuals of which it is composed ... The MAIDSTONE JOURNAL shall continue to support the same principles and conduct it has ever done, and which have recommended it to the liberal encouragement it has experienced, by bearing a firm and steady attachment to the KING and CONSTITUTION.

The paper carried details of elections and of county and town meetings. There were advertisements with offers of employment, and for auctions and house or farm sales, or for patent medicines, and a very limited amount of correspondence, usually signed with a pseudonym. Very infrequently, there was a supplement such as one on the 'Church and King' riots in Birmingham in 1791 or, shortly after the French Revolution, a series on the history of the Bastille.

The *Journal* carried notices of militia men who had not presented themselves for annual training in Maidstone, together with their descriptions, and

in 1791 no less than 37 were listed, six of them Maidstone residents. Absence carried a penalty of £20 or six months' imprisonment and a reward was offered for the apprehension of individuals. News of Maidstone itself was very limited, although the *Journal* regularly included prices in Maidstone market for agricultural produce.

In the 18th and 19th centuries ragstone was used for roadworks, for the sea defences at the Isle of Sheppey, and for Dymchurch Wall protecting Romney Marsh. The state of the streets and lanes of Maidstone was such that in 1790 the Corporation decided to carry out major improvements. The cost of paving, lighting, draining and cleaning the principal roads was estimated at £9,000, and the annual expense thereafter was expected to amount to £750. To meet the cost of the work it was proposed to levy a rate of 1s. 6d. on all householders, half to be paid by the landlord and half by the tenant, and there were to be tollgates at the four main entrances to the town. These propositions were incorporated in the Maidstone Paving Bill which was introduced to Parliament in 1791. The townspeople remained opposed to the payment of tolls, and local opposition led to the proposal for tollgates being dropped, but the measures were otherwise approved and received the royal assent in an Act for

> widening, improving, regulating, paving, cleansing and lighting the streets, lanes and other public passages and places in Maidstone; for removing and preventing encroachments, obstructions, nuisances, and annoyances therein; for the better supplying the town with water; and for repaving and maintaining the highways within the parish.

51   *John Blake (1779-1840), by Samuel Drummond.*
(PCF KTMM 2/02 012).

Commissioners of Pavements, who consisted of the town's Members of Parliament, the

Corporation, and some freeholders and substantial ratepayers, were appointed to oversee the work, but it was principally the Town Council which was involved in practical day-to-day decisions. By 1793 the town was paved, drained and lighted. Street scavenging and the collection of household refuse were introduced, and the butchering of animals in the streets was forbidden. The original conduit for the town's water supply, which had been located in the High Street, was removed as part of the street improvements. The water supply from the spring at Rockyhill had become inadequate for the increased population, and those who could afford to had water piped to their homes from the main supply or made use of private wells.

At times of poor harvests and the consequent price increases in basic foods, it was seen by the mayor and gentry as essential that special measures were taken to avoid famine and the possibility of riots. In December 1794 a subscription was opened by the mayor for the purpose of supplying the poor of the parish of Maidstone with flour at a reduced rate. The *Maidstone Journal* reported that more than £250 had been collected and yet more was expected, and it was anticipated that relief could be provided for the following two months and some 900 families could be assisted in this way. The paper noted 'the spirit of emulation among the nobility and gentry in efforts to outvie in charitable donations for the poor'. In January 1795 the mayor called a meeting to consider a subscription for the purchase of coals for the poor.

Correspondence between Thomas Poole the Mayor of Maidstone and the Privy Council in July and August indicated there was little wheat available throughout the county. The mayor asked for assistance, but none was forthcoming, and he was advised to purchase wheat on the London market. In January 1796 Lord and Lady Romney

52   *Granary, Waterside, demolished in 1992.*

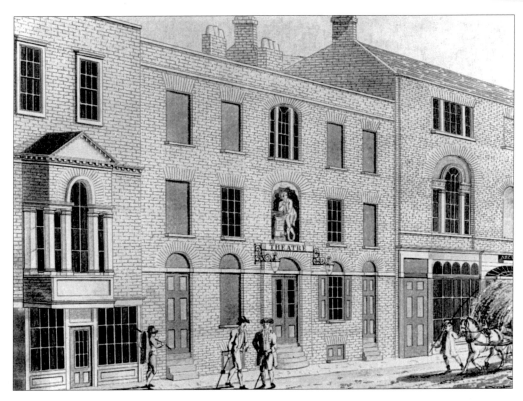

53   *Sarah Baker's theatre, High Street, 1798.*

were reported as helping the poor of the town with liberal gifts, including 40 chaldrons of coal. In the same month the mayor called a meeting at which he urged the townspeople to follow the example of Parliament, the Corporation and the justices and reduce their consumption of wheat by one third.

Markets had been the place since medieval times where the public regulation of commercial transactions, such as the testing of weights and measures and the assize (the fixing of the price) of bread, was carried out. A key factor for consumers had always been the price of a bushel of corn, but this measure was going out of fashion in the latter part of the 18th century. Earl Romney sought to revive it in 1796 and the corn was conveyed to Maidstone market

with due ceremony. The *Gentleman's Magazine* recorded that 'the first parcel was drawn by a good old-fashioned team of English oxen, truly emblematic of the days of yore, and highly gratifying to the inhabitants of that town'. No one was allowed to purchase more than a single bushel.

In 1796 Sarah Baker, a theatrical manager, opened a theatre in the High Street at which her own company performed. She had others at Canterbury, Deal, Rochester and Tunbridge Wells. In time of war the plays presented at her theatres were frequently patriotic and were patronised by the military. On Easter Monday 1797 the Maidstone season commenced with a performance which was attended by the town's Volunteer Regiment.

New industries and commercial ventures appeared in the town towards the end of the century. George Bishop, a native of Maidstone and mayor in 1777 and 1786, had gained experience of distilling gin in Holland and in 1789 he obtained parliamentary approval for a distillery in the town, which he situated on the south side of Bank Street. His production of Hollands gin, or Geneva, was widely acclaimed and he had a warehouse in Leadenhall Street in London for its distribution. A contemporary writer, Walter Rowles, reported that seven hundred hogs were kept on the grains from the distillery. Hollands gin was so popular partly because an Act of Parliament allowed it to be produced at 83° proof. Bishop's advertisement described his gin as 'Sold at the lawful strength, he being allowed by Law to sell Spirits stronger than any other Person'. It was priced at 5s. 9d. a gallon, 3d. more than the English gin which Bishop also produced. In wartime the price of his Hollands gin was increased to 7s. 0d.

The Kentish Bank was founded in Maidstone in 1793 with five prominent local men, Brenchley, Stacey, Parker, Springate and Penfold, as partners. A second bank, the Maidstone County Bank, commenced business with three Maidstone partners, Sir William Bishop, Larkin and Hughes. The Maidstone Bank was formed with Edmeads, Atkins and Tyrell as partners, and the Kent Insurance Company commenced business in Maidstone in 1802.

Justifying an increase to 4d. in the price of the *Maidstone Journal* in 1793, Blake blamed the rise on the decision of the Stamp Office to charge duty on newspapers which were printed but unsold, and 'the great expence in collecting Materials, from a Number of London and Foreign Papers, daily published, as well as, in obtaining Original Intelligence from several Correspondents'.

A Loyalist Association had been formed with government support in London in 1792 and local Associations were set up throughout the country. Maidstone's mayor, Flint Stacey, was a staunch loyalist but, initially, he declined to set up an Association, boasting that 'this town is without any association or meetings tending to destroy the constitution or government, and I never knew the town more tranquil and unanimous than at present'. Only seven days later, however, he was concerned about the selling of radical publications in the town and the display of radical handbills in public houses and other public places and he instructed the town's Recorder to raise the matter with John Reeves, the leader of the London Association. He suggested that 'it [may] be proper to employ a few stout fellows to pull down their papers, and knock down any fellows employed in such treasonable practices … I hope that I shall stand excused for the suggestion, as I mean well'. The mayor reported that he had caused the seditious literature to be withdrawn and his own printed papers were up in every one of the 45 inns within his jurisdiction. Within a short time 'he had effectively curbed the few discontented spirits … and they did not dare to show their heads'. One week later a Loyalist Association was set up in Maidstone, Earl Romney, the Lord Lieutenant, being present at the inaugural meeting.

Maidstone citizens were patriotic and prepared to make a contribution to the defence of the country. Once the Duke of Dorset had persuaded a county meeting held on Penenden Heath in 1794 that individuals should finance and set up Volunteer units to defend the county, no difficulty was experienced in forming the Maidstone Volunteers. Every man was required to provide his own horse and arms and within a few days £200 had been collected in the town to support the unit.

There was also powerful radical and anti-government feeling in Maidstone, one of the town's MPs, Clement Taylor Smythe, a paper manufacturer, being among those holding such views. At a meeting in Maidstone in 1795, open to all townspeople and chaired by the Earl of Thanet, Earl Stanhope spoke against the continuance of the war and the Treason and Sedition bills, and a petition was begun. A similar meeting in 1797 was described by the *Maidstone Journal* as 'the most numerous and respectable meeting of this town and parish ever yet remembered', and the London *Morning Chronicle* reported that there were 3,000 present. A motion referred to 'the calamitous effects of a War unparalleled in the British annals' and its adverse impact on the economy, and called upon the King to dismiss his Ministers. The chairman, Clement Taylor's brother, indicated that the motion was carried by a majority of twenty to one, but this did not prevent the mayor, recorder, jurats, common councillors and 'other inhabitants' from meeting at the *Bull Inn*, under the chairmanship of R. Parker, and approving an Address to the King on lines entirely contrary to those endorsed by the main meeting.

In the long-established industry of papermaking a trade union was making its presence felt. The *Maidstone Journal* in February 1796 expressed the view that:

> It is very greatly to be feared, that the frequent occurrence of attempts among artificers, of various descriptions to increase the price of their labour –

will, if not effectively resisted, eventually lead to the Ruin of the Manufactures of this Kingdom. We are lead into this observation, from finding that, the whole of the very extensive Paper Manufactory, of this County, is at present, entirely at a stand; owing to a combination among the Workmen, to obtain a very great advance upon the ample Wages they now receive.

The report goes on to praise the spirited actions which the manufacturers were taking to combat the workers' efforts, but the Master Papermakers of Maidstone and District were, in fact, unable to resist the demands of the Original Society of Papermakers. The union successfully resisted reductions in wages and even obtained increases in March 1796.

In the same year, John Gale Jones of the London Corresponding Society, the leading radical body, paid a visit to Maidstone. He was entertained by Clement Taylor Smythe and meetings chaired by Smythe's brother were held at the *Castle Inn*, a venue patronised by radicals. The loyalists used the Star Coffeehouse as their rendezvous and neither group ventured on to the other's territory for fear of meeting with a rebuff. A radical Corresponding Society was set up in the town following Jones's visit but neither Loyalist Association nor Corresponding Society endured for long. The Loyalist Association had effectively ended by the end of 1793 whilst the Corresponding Society did not last beyond 1800.

A handbill designed to encourage insurrection was distributed to troops stationed in Maidstone by Henry Fellows in 1797, although it is far from clear whether he had the support of the London Corresponding Society, as was alleged. He was arrested, charged with seeking to suborn the troops, sentenced to two years' imprisonment,

54　*Mote Park, the Romney family estate, is now open to the public.*

and required to find two securities of £250 for his subsequent behaviour.

The King supporting his troops provided a rallying point for patriotism, and in August 1799 Mote Park, the home of Lord Romney, hosted an event at which George III, accompanied by his family and by government ministers, reviewed a parade and manoeuvres by the combined Kent Volunteers. The whole assembly marched into town with drums beating, bands playing and colours flying and, according to the newspapers, 'the loyalty shewn by the inhabitants of Maidstone, was truly conspicuous'. The largest single infantry unit was the Maidstone Volunteers. After the Inspection 5,258 Volunteers sat down to dinner. There was

an ample supply of port, 16 butts of ale and as much small beer, and a pump communicating with the cellar was fixed outside the house 'for the purpose of obtaining what more might be necessary'. The Review inspired a poem, 'The Lord of the Mote', which was published in the *Gentleman's Magazine*, and the Volunteers were so impressed by what Romney had done that they paid for a stone pavilion to be erected in Mote Park as a tribute to him.

An important wartime treason trial took place at Maidstone. Four Irishmen were arrested in 1798 having travelled by boat from London to the North Kent coast, where they attempted to hire another boat to take them to France. Principal among the accused were O'Coigley, a

Catholic priest, and O'Connor, a Dublin editor. Pending the trial, the prisoners were kept in Maidstone gaol and the government sent more than 300 troops from Canterbury to Maidstone to guard it. It is possible this was a psychological move, a show of strength in a town with some radical sympathies.

O'Coigley was duly found guilty and hung, drawn and quartered. O'Connor was acquitted, having brought as character witnesses the Duke of Norfolk, the Earl of Thanet, Richard Brinsley Sheridan and Charles James Fox, the leader of the Opposition Whigs in Parliament. But no sooner was O'Connor acquitted than he was re-arrested on another charge, whereupon the Earl of Thanet drew his sword and attempted to rescue him from the clutches of the law. For this he was sentenced to one year's imprisonment in the Tower of London

and a fine of £1,000. O'Connor eventually confessed his guilt but managed to escape to France, where he served for a time as a Lieutenant-General in the French Army.

Food shortages and resulting high prices for bread, the basic commodity consumed by the poor, caused particular problems throughout the country around the turn of the century. The Maidstone price for a gallon of wheat in 1782 had been 10d. but by 1799 it had risen to 2s. 1d. A quartern loaf in 1788 was 6d. to 8d., whilst in 1794 it was 11d. to 12d. The only formal way of funding poor relief was by way of the poor rate, and in the 20 years between 1783 and 1803 the level at which the rate was levied in Maidstone increased by 70 per cent. It seems that Maidstone was better off in this respect than other nearby towns, however. In Rochester the increase

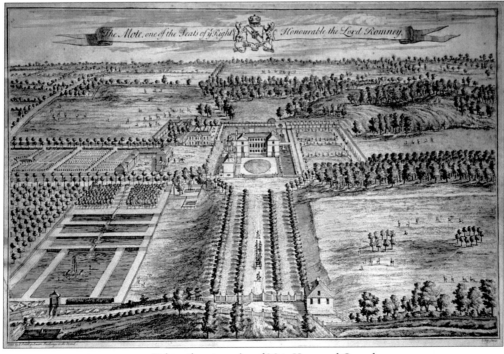

55   *Eighteenth-century plan of Mote House and Grounds.*

56   *Cricket match played in Maidstone, c.1800.*

had been 150 per cent and in Chatham 200 per cent. Even in Canterbury the increase was 100 per cent.

The food shortages of 1800 produced riots throughout the country and Maidstone was not entirely immune. In October of that year numbers of men assembled in the Market Place and hissed and hooted the farmers. The mayor and justices threatened to read the Riot Act but the mob proceeded to break the windows of Mr Burgess's house (George Burgess became mayor in 1809), and treated him in 'a shameful manner'. The price of a quartern loaf in Maidstone by this time varied between 1s. 1d. and 1s. 3¾d., more than twice what it had been 10 or 12 years previously. Public subscriptions in the town provided for some 1,500 portions of 'an excellent and nutritious

soup at 1d. per quart', 1,500 quarts having been made at a cost of 12 guineas. Three thousand poor people were supplied with flour at the reduced price of 1s. 6d. a gallon.

Cricket was played in Kent in the 18th century and there is a record of matches being played at Maidstone at the turn of the next century. In May 1801 the Master Papermakers held a meeting at the *Star Inn* at which they praised 'the Act now pending in Parliament, for the effectual Suppression of Combinations', and expressed their determination to enforce the Act, when passed, 'with the utmost Rigour'. Although the Combination Act 1801 had the effect of making trade unions illegal, it was largely ineffective, and the Papermakers' Union was again able to secure increases in that year, in spite of the employers' threats.

Six

Industry and Commerce, the Poor and Riots, 1804-1850

In July 1804 there were again disturbances in the town arising from the high cost of foodstuffs. The Riot Act was read and several of the demonstrators were arrested. A troop of horse was sent for and order was restored. Cavalry barracks had been erected in 1797 at the end of Week Street, and 20 officers and more than 300 rank and file of the Yeomanry Cavalry of Kent were on permanent duty for 12 days in a successful attempt to keep the situation under control. The cost of the exercise was £535 14s. 6d., and the War Office was eventually persuaded to relieve the town of this financial burden, although it was not until six years later, in August 1810, that the bill was settled.

Out of the trust funds of Duke's Charity, which had been set up prior to 1736 and which owned land in Romney Marsh and elsewhere, three almshouses were erected around the turn of the century to add to those the trust had already provided for single women who worshipped at the Presbyterian (later Unitarian) church. In 1805 Ann Wright gave the interest on £1,100 of 3 per cent annuities to be divided among 30 needy widows or single women of Maidstone.

Paper making began to modernise in the early years of the 19th century and the smaller mills, operating with water power and with little in the way of machinery and still making paper by hand, were unable to compete with the larger mills. Balston's Springfield Mill was equipped with papermaking machinery and, in 1806, was the first paper mill in Kent to be steam-powered.

The Kent Fire Office, formerly the Kent Insurance Company, acquired a manual fire engine which was kept in All Saints' churchyard until 1820. The Pavement Commissioners then erected an engine house large enough to accommodate two engines near the river bridge. The Kent Life Assurance Company was founded in 1806, and in 1823 it became part of the Fire Office. 'White collar' employment in the town had begun to appear, with jobs in insurance, local and national government and the Post Office, but it was not until later in the century that it would assume significant proportions.

The early 1800s saw a growth in trade unionism among skilled workers. Apart from the papermakers' union, which was well established

57   *West side of Week Street, c.1800.*

and moved its headquarters from St. Paul's Cray to Maidstone in 1815, the United Friendly Society of Bricklayers was formed in Maidstone in 1810. A general strike among Maidstone building workers in 1825 brought wage increases for mechanics, carpenters, plumbers and bricklayers.

At the census in 1811 the number of inhabitants of the town was 9,443, 404 houses having been erected in the previous ten years. Within another decade the number had increased to 12,508, living in 2,131 houses, with a further 103 houses uninhabited at this time. The main centres of habitation remained the High Street, Union Street, Week Street, Stone Street and King Street. Housing on the other side of the Medway had expanded, more than 300 buildings now being situated in the West Borough and at Tovil.

Maidstone continued to be a military centre and in 1813 the barracks were being used as the army's training school for young horses. Until the Napoleonic Wars came to an end in 1815 the town was full of soldiers either stationed there or passing through en route to mainland Europe, the West Indies or India. In June 1814 the encampment at Coxheath was closed by Act of Parliament and was no longer available to accommodate troops. The Riding School was transferred in 1833 to Maidstone barracks, which also served as the depôt for cavalry regiments serving in India.

The Presbyterian Market Street congregation had, in large part, become Arian by 1745, but changed its allegiance once more in 1813. By this time the law had changed and it was no longer blasphemous to deny the Trinity, so it declared itself Unitarian, regarding Christ as merely a divinely inspired human being whose death was not atonement for human sins.

The *Maidstone Gazette* was first published in 1815 and continued under a variety of titles. It followed the *Maidstone Journal* in proclaiming its political allegiance when, in 1830, the editor wrote, 'The success which attends the course of the *Maidstone Gazette* we feel convinced is mainly attributable to the integrity and consistency of its principles ... Tory we are, Tory we still are and Tory we shall remain.'

An alternative to passenger travel by road between London and Maidstone by 1816 was a regular boat service operated on the Thames between London and Gravesend, from whence there was a connecting bus service to Maidstone. The Kentish Bank was forced to cease operations in March of that year due to the failure to meet their commitments of its London agents, Ramsbottom & Co. The Maidstone County Bank suffered a similar fate when its London agents, Bruce, Simpson & Co., also defaulted on their commitments, and the Maidstone Bank closed down in 1825 for a similar reason. The Kentish Bank was reformed, and renamed the New Kentish bank, by three prominent Maidstone residents: Corrall, a hop-grower, Homewood, a local JP, and Mercer, a miller. It opened for business in the High Street with a tenancy agreement which read:

> Messrs. Corrall, Homewood and Mercer agree with Mr John Mercer to hire the New Kentish

58 *Entrance to Army Barracks, Sandling Road, no longer in existence.*

59   *Gasholder, St Peter's Street.*

Bank for seventeen years containing the front room for the Bank, and a room to put the safe in and one back office with the best stairs and all the landing place with three sleeping rooms over the Bank and two over the gateway and a room over the safe at a yearly rent of fifty pounds.

When George Bishop died in 1818 his distillery came into the hands of his relatives. Their mismanagement meant the business had to be sold, but in 1819, when Argles Bishop applied for a licence to run a rival distillery in St Peters Street, the Excise Office took the opportunity to close down both distilleries on the grounds that the Act permitting Bishop's distillery had become inoperative since the original business had changed hands. The premises behind Bank Street were then converted into a flour mill. In 1818 Ann Willes, then residing at Dulwich, left a will in which she gave to the trustees of Duke's Charity £1,000 of 3 per cent annuities, the interest to be divided among the six residents of the almshouses. By 1834 the annual income of the Drake/Willes trust amounted to £191 8s.

60   *The Market Place, High Street, 1820.*

61 *Market day in the High Street, 1822.*

Although the 1791 Paving Act had included provision for improvements to the water supply, it was not until 1819 that any significant changes were made. The Commissioners laid down new iron pipes and installed 17 conduits from the spring at Rockyhill. Sarah Barker, who had been a successful impresario throughout Kent, died in 1815 and her theatres were taken over by William Dowton, her son-in-law and a well-known comedian. Their popularity declined and in 1839 the Baker theatrical circuit came to an end. The Maidstone theatre was demolished in 1851.

By 1821 the population had increased to 12,508, and ten years later the figure had reached 15,387. In 1841 the number of inhabitants of the parish was 17,805, much of the increase attributable to births outnumbering deaths, a smaller proportion to the influx of people from neighbouring villages seeking employment in the town.

Maidstone's streets were unlit and dangerous until, in 1822, a contract was entered into with what was to become the Gas, Light & Coke Company to install gas lighting to public areas of the town. Almost two hundred gas lamps were fitted and Maidstone became unusually well lit for a country town at this time. The markets were removed from the High Street in 1825 and replaced by new buildings adjacent to the *Mitre Hotel*. The monthly cattle market was removed to Fair Meadow, but the new markets were never entirely successful. After their removal from the High Street, market stalls found it difficult to compete with the retail shops now widespread throughout the town. The places where the stalls had stood were often occupied by offices.

A new prison was completed by 1819 behind County Hall and a new court house was erected in front of the prison in 1826. The gallows on Penenden Heath had been the source of complaints by residents of the area, and in August 1819 they again urged the magistrates

62 *Maidstone Prison entrance.*

63 *Old Assize Courts,
Week Street.*

64 *Maidstone Prison wall was
one mile in circumference.*

to remove executions to the front of the new gaol. They complained that:

> Our properties on the days when these unfortunate men are to forfeit their lives is much injured, the mob after the execution operating *interrorum* [to terrify] it is actually by many of the workmen and apprentices considered a day of pleasure.

Their representations had no immediate effect, but in June 1831 Lord Baden Powell requested the magistrates to change the venue for hangings to the top of the gateway of the prison and his request was endorsed by the High Sheriff. The two men urged that there were serious objections to the existing arrangements:

> Not only as it affects the morals of the persons who are drawn together to witness the execution by many of whom it seems rather to be considered as affording an opportunity for dissipation and vice than as presenting an awful and salutary warning but especially as it affects the unhappy criminal whose mind is too frequently distracted during the procession of not less than a mile from that attention to his spiritual adviser to which the last hours of his life ought to be continually devoted.

The magistrates eventually concurred with the proposal. The last execution on Penenden Heath took place in December 1830 and the first in front of the gaol in August 1831. The place of execution was moved inside the prison walls in 1868.

The Catholic Emancipation Bill proceeding through Parliament in 1828 provoked strong opposition in Kent, and in Maidstone in particular. What was said to be one of the largest meetings ever held on Penenden Heath condemned it. One of the leaders of the opposition was Sir John Wells, a Maidstone Member of Parliament, who declared that he was prepared to fight 'in defence of the glorious

Protestant Constitution' until he was 'up to his knees in blood'. The Maidstone newspapers strongly urged rejection of the Bill and an initial meeting of the Brunswick Society, created solely to oppose Catholic emancipation, was held at the *Bell Inn*, but so great was the throng that it had to be adjourned to the Town Hall.

In the late 1820s and early 1830s expenditure on the workhouse was 3s. 8d. a week per head, privatisation having resulted in savings of £1,000. In 1830 a dispensary was opened to serve those poor who became ill. A small building was leased and four doctors gave their services without payment. Public financial support easily surpassed the cost of the project, and two years later plans were launched for a more grandiose scheme. By 1833 the West Kent General Hospital was opened with accommodation for 24 patients.

The Swing Riots of the 1830s, mainly of agricultural workers, were principally located in rural areas of Kent, Maidstone being one of the few towns where their effects were felt directly. It was reported to the Home Office that the town was 'infested with radicals, chiefly journeymen artificers'. On 29 October 1830 John Adams, a Maidstone cobbler, led some 300 men to Sir John Filmer's farm at East Sutton. Acting as a spokesman, Adams expressed their grievances and asked for money 'for refreshments'. Filmer gave him two guineas. The same evening the mob descended upon the Rev. James Gambler, Rector of Langley, who gave Adams one guinea in response to his demand. The following day an even larger group was intent upon marching on Maidstone, but the magistrates and a troop of soldiers met it just outside the town and the ringleaders were arrested. Robert Peel, the Home

65 *West Kent Hospital in Marsham Street was closed in 1983.*

Secretary, fearing trouble in the town, ordered two pieces of artillery to be sent to Maidstone, but in the event they were not needed.

In the first decade of the 1800s there were 25 barges on the River Medway, carrying goods to and from Maidstone. By 1834 there were more than 50 vessels of up to 90 tons, but the river traffic was facing competition from road transport, horse-drawn heavy goods wagons now circulating on all the main roads; by 1835 even these vehicles were being superseded by light lorries.

Directories of the 1830s indicate that there were seven coaches a day from Maidstone to London and a similar number to the Medway towns. Maidstone appears to have had more van services operating from it in 1839 than any other town apart from Canterbury. There were also many more carriers operating from Maidstone than from elsewhere in the county, and this was a pattern which appears to have remained constant throughout the remainder of the 19th century.

A Select Committee was appointed by Parliament in 1833 to examine the working of municipal corporations and recommend any necessary changes. It concluded that a Royal Commission should conduct a full-scale enquiry into the matter, and *The Times* heartily endorsed the need for the Commission when it wrote that 'the most active spring of election bribery and villainy everywhere is known to be the corporation system'. Maidstone was one of only five towns in the whole of England and Wales which refused to co-operate with the Commission, the town clerk and deputy recorder advising the Corporation that it was contrary both to common law and to the statute law of the realm.

Two of the Commissioners investigated Maidstone and, acknowledging that in the circumstances their report was bound to be deficient, produced a damning indictment:

> It is not easy to imagine a greater perversion of municipal institutions, than a system under which bribes are given for the purpose of escaping from the highest office, and under which that office is inflicted as a measure of hostility ... [This represents] purely the effects of political party spirit, which prevails with the utmost rancour

66 *Benjamin Disraeli MP (1882), by Sidney Hodges*
(PCF KTMM 2/01 016).

67 *The original 1836 proposal for a railway station in the High Street, which was never built following opposition from the Corporation.*

and bitterness of feeling. Both parties go to the contest with the object only of showing their strength and annoying their opponents.

The Mayor of Maidstone was allowed only £5 to meet expenses, although it cost him between £100 and £200, principally in providing a breakfast for the town's 'respectable inhabitants' on his final day in office, so it is hardly surprising that individuals sought to avoid appointment to that particular office. There were even occasions when bribery was employed to avoid becoming mayor. The Commissioners' adverse comments on the freemen of the town demonstrated their middle-class prejudices:

> It is scarcely to be expected that the proceedings of a body, composed as the freemen are, would be regulated by considerations of the well-being of the town. The result has been that, where the decision of a question is not influenced by bribery, the issue most commonly depends upon the popular feeling prevalent among the lowest classes at the time, and is independent of the merits.

The Coxheath Union was created in the year following the Poor Law Amendment Act 1834, with the intention that it should take the place of workhouses in all neighbouring areas. The Maidstone Trustees of the Poor had been strongly opposed to the legislation and petitioned against it, and in 1836 rejected the idea of being included with rural parishes at Coxheath. But the Commissioners' views prevailed and Maidstone became part of what was then renamed the Maidstone Union. Maidstone inmates were removed to Coxheath and the workhouse in Knightrider Street was sold.

Benjamin Disraeli was a successful candidate at the 1837 General Election in Maidstone. He had changed his name from D'Israeli by omitting the apostrophe in his election address, and so it remained thereafter. At the next election he decided to stand as a candidate at Shrewsbury, unable to afford the expense of what he described as 'the cupidity of the electors of Maidstone'.

In 1836 it had been proposed that the railway from London to Dover should go by way of Maidstone, but this was resisted by the Corporation, which argued that the railway would be detrimental to the trade of the town. In 1844 a branch line was opened from Maidstone to Paddock Wood, from where it was possible to transfer to trains for London. In 1856 the line was extended beyond Maidstone to Strood, where it linked up with the North Kent Railway, which also ran trains to London.

Although thread making had come to an end around 1812, 88 townspeople were engaged in making hop bags, ropes and blankets, according to the census in 1831. James Clifford was the principal manufacturer of hop bagging and jute pocketing in the 1840s in what had previously been the workhouse building.

The Strood to Gravesend Canal opened in 1824, reducing the journey from Maidstone to London by some 25 miles, and as a consequence there was an increase in river traffic. In the long run, however, this was not able to compete with land transport, whether by lorry or by train, and the canal was not used as such after the 1840s, the canal tunnel becoming part of the rail route to Strood.

A tiny borough police force had been created by 1820 but it proved ineffectual. In 1837 it was

68 *Corrall's Almshouses, 1845, in College Road.*

replaced by a force numbering 11 officers, and a police station was opened in King Street in 1841. At first only the area within three-quarters of a mile of the Town Hall was patrolled, and inhabitants residing within it had to pay a supplementary rate for the privilege.

In 1845 the Corrall Charity, provided for by the will of Mrs Carter, erected six almshouses in Orchard Lane for three male and three female householders in reduced circumstances. Each house was endowed with £15 a year. In 1846 John Woolcott, an oculist in the town, undertook to provide eye treatment to those who could not afford to pay. A public subscription that year allowed an Ophthalmic Hospital to be founded, Lord Romney purchasing an old school building in Church Street for the purpose and letting it out at a nominal rent.

Maidstone's average death rate in the period 1838-44 was 23.7 (male) and 22.1 (female) people per 1,000, which was lower than the national average, but the town could not escape the epidemics which swept the country from time to time. A cholera outbreak in 1849 resulted in 43 deaths, almost all of them vagrant Irish hop pickers, but around this time serious consideration was being given to reducing the health hazards to which the town's population was exposed. John Whichcord, the mayor in 1847, was active in the campaign to improve the sanitary condition. He was strongly supported by Dr Francis Plomley, the medical officer to the Maidstone Poor Law Union who, in the early part of 1848, published in the *Maidstone Gazette* a series of letters on the subject. A public meeting asked for a government inspector to carry out an enquiry into how improvements could be made. A Local Board of Health was not established, as it could have been under the 1848 Health Act, but the council did appoint an Inspector of Nuisances.

SEVEN

Industrial Expansion and Town Developments, 1851-1900

In 1851 the Corporation took further steps towards the creation of a healthier environment in the town. With a loan of £5,000 from the Public Works Loan Board, it built public baths, wash-houses and a swimming pool on the Fair Meadow. The swimming pool proved to be popular but there was little demand for the other facilities and these were closed in 1858.

The Watch Committee adopted the Lodging House Act in 1851, which enabled it to exercise some control over lodging houses in the town. Of the 35 premises which were then approved, 15 were public houses. But, despite the increased supervision allowed by the Act, the poor condition of lodging houses remained a matter of concern until well into the following century. In the same year a more suitable building became available to the Ophthalmic Hospital, paid for in part by the £500 raised by public subscription. With the wider facilities then available it became possible for working-class people in the county to receive eye treatment in return for a contribution of 1d. a week.

Schools in the town had multiplied in number in the 19th century, and by 1851 there were 30 day

schools open to all. Eight of these were endowed schools and 19 were church schools, most of them linked to the Church of England. The church schools charged pupils 1d. or 2d. a week, at least until the 1870s. A Census of Religious Worship in 1851 showed that the predominant religion in the town was the Church of England. All Saints' had an attendance of around 2,000 whilst Holy Trinity (founded in 1828) had more than 1,000. Attendances at St Peter (1840) and St Stephen (1841) were probably less than 100. Among dissenters, Wesleyan Methodists (1823) and the Countess of Huntington's Connexion (1831) had some 300 to 500 worshippers, Independents (1822), General Baptists, Providence (1830), King Street (1822) and Particular Baptists (1834) all had attendances numbering between 100 and 300. Attendances at chapels of Presbyterians or Unitarians (1736), Society of Friends (1811) and Primitive Methodists (1832) were insignificant. Rather more than 22 per cent of the town's population were at church or chapel for the morning service. The Roman Catholic church of St Francis in Week Street, close by the Sessions House, is not included in the census as it was

69 *Map of the town of Maidstone in the county of Kent, 1848.*

MAP

OF THE TOWN OF

MAIDSTONE

IN THE COUNTY OF

KENT,

1848.

PUBLISHED BY J. TOOTELL, SURVEYOR, MAIDSTONE.

Scale of Chains.

70   *Public baths and washhouses on the Fair Meadow, 1851.*

71   *All Saints' School in College Road.*

72 Holy Trinity Church, Church Street, was created a parish in 1841.

73 St Peter's Church, St Peter's Street. The original mid-13th-century chapel of the hospital, founded by Archbishop Boniface, was enlarged into a parish church in 1836-7 (above right).

74 Wesleyan Chapel, Union Street, 1823 (right).

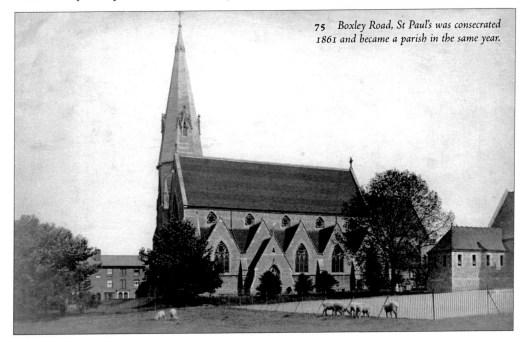

75 Boxley Road, St Paul's was consecrated 1861 and became a parish in the same year.

not founded until 1859. Towards the end of the century there were 10 Church of England churches and 13 others catering for various forms of nonconformism.

Distilling was resumed in the town in 1853 when Grant's Cherry Brandy Company moved from Dover to Hart Street, near the railway station in the West Borough. Apart from Cherry Brandy, Hollands gin was produced there and the company also imported foreign wines and spirits. In the papermaking industry, trade unionism spread beyond the Original Society of Papermakers in 1854 when another craft union, the United Brotherhood of Papermakers, was founded for machine mill workers. This subsequently became the Amalgamated Society of Papermakers. The Boot and Shoemakers Union, the Compositors and Printers, and the Stonemakers all had branches in the town by this date.

When the Kent County Constabulary was formed in 1857 the headquarters were situated at Wren's Cross on Stone Street and Maidstone barracks was used to drill the police recruits. In the first eight months of the constabulary's existence almost one third of the force resigned or were dismissed, some 40 per cent of offences being connected with drink. The borough force remained a separate entity until the mid-20th century.

Maidstone was not a major barge-building centre but numbers of barges had been built in the previous century. The 40-ton *Defiance*, built at Maidstone as early as 1789, was still in service at Sittingbourne 140 years later. Barge building on a small scale continued into the 1850s, with barges of up to 90 tons being built. In 1859 a further newspaper became available when the

76   *Boatyard on the River Medway.*

first Maidstone edition of the *Kent Messenger* was published. The newspaper has continued to the present day.

The inadequacy of the supply of water continued to cause concern. The councillors would have preferred the Pavement Commissioners, rather than a private company, to control the supply of the town's water but the ratepayers rejected this proposal for a second time in 1858 and a private company, the Maidstone Water Company, was incorporated by Act of Parliament in 1860. The company obtained spring water

77   *Coasting barge on the Medway.*

from the ragstone running alongside the railway line to Paddock Wood, and this was piped to a new pumping station outside the town at East Farleigh Bridge. From there it went to a reservoir at Barming, from whence it was supplied to the town. The company's remit required it to fill the town's reservoirs, supply water for street cleaning, and situate fire hydrants adjacent to the new water mains.

In harsh winters, when food was both scarce and relatively costly, a subscription relief fund was initiated by the mayor to help the poor, the sick and the unemployed. The years 1855-7 saw particularly bad winters and relief funds were used to provide soup kitchens.

Sanitary arrangements occupied the minds of the Pavement Commissioners throughout the 1850s and 1860s. Although it was recognised

78 *The present-day Museum, from St Faiths Street. It is hoped (2008) to provide improved facilities by developing the east wing.*

that pollution from paper and oil mills, and particularly from the town's sewage, constituted a health hazard, the cost of installing sewers and drains led to constant prevarication on the part of the authorities. In 1860 around a quarter of houses had no sewers, mostly in poorer areas where streets were neither paved nor lit, but by 1864 some progress had been made with improvements. The River Len sewer had been completed and a main sewer was installed in the High Street with connections to Tonbridge Road, but two more years elapsed before the newly created Local Board of Health was able to draw up a comprehensive scheme of drains and sewers. Its implementation was further delayed by a dispute with the Local Government Board about how the necessary money was to be raised.

In 1858 Thomas Charles of Chillington House bequeathed to the town his collection of antiquities, together with books and pictures. His former residence was purchased by the Corporation and opened as a museum. The first curator, Edward Pretty, left the museum a considerable collection of books and drawings in 1865, and in 1867 a room in the museum was assigned to the Kent Archaeological Society and its collection was, and remains, housed there.

There was trouble in the town in 1862 when rival gangs of hoppers numbering around a thousand gathered near Maidstone West station. According to the *Maidstone Gazette*, 'showers of stones were hurled by the women ... the men using their shillelaghs and bagging hooks in a most determined manner'. Twenty-four of the mob were injured, including a baby who later died. The police were present but felt unable to intervene, and the fact that the size of the force was increased, so that by 1869 it numbered 23 officers, may be related. The patrolled area was enlarged and the police, in addition to dealing with crime, were charged with the inspection of lodging houses and with the accuracy of weights and measures.

In 1865 Thomas Cutbush provided six almshouses in Church Street, each endowed with £52, for decayed, married tradesmen who had carried on business in the town for at least 20 years, or for artisans over 60 years of age who had been employed for the same length of time. Two years later he founded another charity for 12 widows or spinsters aged more than 50 years who had lived in the town for 20 years; each of them was to receive £26 a year.

A further step towards the provision of a healthier environment was the appointment of a part-time medical officer for the town in 1868, followed by the full-time appointment of Dr M.A. Adams in 1875. Among the improvements he encouraged were the repair and replacement of house drains and a reduction in the use of cesspools. The scheme for the disposal of sewage which had begun in 1864 was not completed until 1879, when the drainage system was finalised and a sewage works constructed at Allington.

The east and west wings adjoining Chillington House had not been included in the Corporation's original purchase but were later purchased with financial assistance from Alexander Randall, Julius Brenchley and Samuel Mercer. In 1869 Brenchley donated part of his collection of birds, shells and insects to the museum, and on

79 *Cutbush Almshouses, College Street.*

80   *Cutbush Almshouses, interior courtyard.*

his death in 1873 his art collection, library and other artefacts were transferred there. A reading room was opened at the same time. In 1874 the Tudor south wing of East Farleigh Court Lodge was re-erected adjacent to the east end of the Museum gallery.

In 1869 Jesse Ellis began a business which expanded rapidly. He started as a haulage contractor but by 1882 was manufacturing agricultural machinery. By 1885 he had moved to St Peters Street, where his premises included a railway siding and a wharf. He held a patent for hop-growing equipment and was also engaged in road repair work for the County Council.

Elections in Maidstone were dominated by party allegiances. The pollbooks in 1865 show that all but 65 out of 1,696 voters, whether they were Liberal or Conservative, cast their two votes for both their party's candidates. Not only in Maidstone, but throughout virtually the whole of Kent, dissenting ministers voted Liberal whilst every Anglican clergyman voted Conservative. Employer-employee relationships may also have had some influence. In the 1870 election the Maidstone stationmaster voted Liberal, as did 40 of the 49 station employees. The deputy-governor of Maidstone gaol voted Conservative, as did all 22 of his staff.

A number of open spaces were made available to the public, Brenchley Gardens, alongside the museum, being donated to the town by Julius Brenchley in 1870. The Archbishop's Palace and its grounds were purchased for the town in 1887, and in the last two decades of the century the council provided sports grounds and playgrounds on Penenden Heath, Barming Heath, Tonbridge Road, Stone Street and Lock Meadow. Allotments were provided for the poor

81 *Brenchley Gardens, the Museum Long Gallery (originally Court Lodge), East Farleigh.*

82 *The Museum, from St Faiths Street, comprising Chillington House (1858) with later additions, including the eastern section of the half-timbered Court Lodge, East Farleigh, which was erected against the east wall of the museum gallery.*

83 *Julius Lucius Brenchley Esq. (1876), by William Charles Thomas Dobson (95.1876).*

84 *Julius Brenchley, aged 35, from a Daguerrotype portrait taken in the Sandwich Islands, 1851.*

on Barming Heath, Scrubbs Lane, Rockyhill and on Hastings Road.

In 1871 one of Maidstone's Members of Parliament, Sir John Lubbock, persuaded Parliament to adopt the Bank Holidays Act. The bank officers in the United Kingdom, as a testimonial to him, raised the sum of almost £700, and Lady Lubbock made a contribution of £100. Sir John requested that the money be divided between Maidstone Grammar School and the City of London College, so the interest on the money was used in Maidstone to institute a free scholarship. Three further scholarships were created by friends of the late Alexander Randall, who had played a leading role in the town and was widely respected. He had been a member of the Town Council from 1835 to 1859 and was High Sheriff of the county in 1861. His popularity is evidenced by the fact that in 1861 a public subscription had raised the sum of 600 guineas towards the painting of his portrait.

In 1871 Thomas Edmett endowed a charity which provided annuities of not more than £20 each to poor persons aged 60 years and upwards, and also provided the means to distribute coals, blankets and warm clothing to the poor. Twelve boys were apprenticed in 1880 from the Fisher Trust, originating in 1671, and numbers of poor widows and others of the deserving poor were also given assistance in winter time. Bread charities alone, many from earlier centuries, provided an income of £144 in 1879, and this provided some relief for those in greatest need. The boys' grammar school was moved to a new building in Tonbridge Road in 1871, whilst in 1884 a grammar school for girls, financed by surplus funds of the Rochester Bridge charity, was situated in Albion Place.

85 *Brenchley Gardens, St Faith's and Museum Gardens (above).*

86 *Original entrance to Brenchley Gardens (left).*

87 *An Edwardian audience at the Bandstand in Brenchley Gardens (below).*

88 *London and County Bank, High Street.*

89   Boys' Grammar School, Tonbridge Road.

90   Girls' Grammar School, Albion Place.

VACNIACÆ

91   *The School of Science and Arts was run privately at the end of the 19th century.*

Twine making had come to an end by 1872 but James Clifford had already turned to hop pockets made from Dundee jute, as well as hop screening made from coir fabric, sails, tarpaulin, coconut matting and rope. His success may have been due, in part, to the employment of convict labour from Maidstone gaol and Canterbury prison, which would have served to keep down his labour costs. There were a number of mineral water manufacturers, the most flourishing being J.W. Maskell in St Peters Street, which was taken over by Courage in the second half of the following century, Walter Hayward in Milton Street, and Daniel Lyle in Church Street.

In 1872 a union for unskilled workers was formed in the town. The Kent and Sussex Labourers' Union was led by Alfred Simmons, a Maidstone journalist who adopted a conciliatory attitude towards industrial conflict rather than resort to strike. An important role which the unions fulfilled was the provision of assistance with emigration to overseas territories. In 1874 the *Dover Express* reported on the efforts of the Kent Agricultural Labourers' Union in assisting emigrants from north-west Kent:

On Thursday evening an entertainment was given in the Corn Exchange, Maidstone, to 410 Kentish immigrants [*sic*], on their departure to New Zealand, to which place they had been granted free passage through the instrumentality of the officers of the above union. On Friday the emigrants marched to the railway station, the High Street being crowded with spectators, and the party left for Gravesend.

92   *Maskell & Son's mineral water factory, St Peter's Street.*

Similar scenes were reported when a later group of 400 emigrants departed for New Zealand.

In 1874 it was decided to replace the bridge over the Medway and plans were prepared by Sir Joseph Bazalgette, the engineer responsible for the construction of the Thames Embankment. The new and larger stone bridge was opened on 6 August 1879 and among those present were five thousand schoolchildren, each wearing a commemorative medal. Flooding continued to occur in a number of areas of the town adjoining the river. A direct rail link from Maidstone to London was constructed and Maidstone East station was opened in 1874.

There were several small engineering and foundry firms operating in the 1840s, but most had ceased business by the 1870s or 1880s. Joseph Brown & Sons continued making pumps and engines until 1872. Garrett & Co., who manufactured agricultural machinery, had moved to Maidstone from Suffolk and by the late 1890s were making printing and papermaking machinery. William Weeks and Son were engaged in general and agricultural engineering in the High Street in 1872 but expanded and removed to the Perseverance Iron Works at Waterside. They suffered financial difficulties but survived into the 20th century. Drake & Muirhead, later Drake & Fletcher, began as engineers in the 1870s but by 1882 had expanded into the Kentish Engineering Works in the West Borough, and in the 1890s were making gas and oil engines and plant for sewage works.

Food manufacture was another burgeoning industry. Ebenezer Steer was engaged in large-

93 *Nineteenth-century housing in West Borough.*

scale jam making and by 1881 produced 1,500 tons from premises in Pudding Lane. Another jam factory was started by Charles Chambers in Hart Street in 1891. Although it employed as many as 150 workers it was not successful and came to an end in 1895. Confectionery was manufactured by Edward Sharp from 1876, originally in his Week Street grocer's shop where the sweets were made by his wife.

A sugar boiler was acquired in 1889 and the business expanded into jellies, custard powder and lemonade powder.

Richard Dann had commenced in 1872 as brass founders and ironmongers and by the 1890s the company had expanded into electrical engineering and was occupying Jesse Ellis's original premises in Union Street. Gardner & Co. were established in the same year as Dann

94 *Opening of railway in 1874, as seen from Week Street/County Road.*

and, like him, were originally brass founders. They operated from the Medway Brass Works at Waterside and by 1882 had expanded into general engineering. By 1898 they were producing beer engines at Brewer Street.

One business which acquired a nationwide reputation was that of George Foster Clark. Clark began by producing baking powder, lemonade powder and self-raising flour at his grocer's shop and in 1891 he acquired small premises in Mote Road and adopted the 'Eiffel Tower' as a trademark. In 1895 he moved to the Chambers jam factory premises and changed the name to the Eiffel Tower Works.

It had been the practice for country banks to issue their own notes, but restrictions introduced in 1844 led to a falling off in the practice. The New Kentish Bank was among the last of the country banks to issue its own banknotes, and this it did until 1888. In 1890 a borough lending library was established, although less than 700 townspeople were eligible to borrow books

since it was necessary to be a ratepayer or to be guaranteed by a ratepayer. In 1897 the Victoria Free Library was erected adjacent to the museum, and it contained a reference section, lending library and newspaper collection.

One of the problems throughout the century was the large numbers of families which descended on the town at the time of hop picking. In 1876, for example, tents were erected on the Fair Meadow and some two thousand men, women and children were accommodated there. Hoppers were also using the casual wards in the workhouse to a limited extent, although harsh conditions encouraged many to prefer to sleep in the streets of the town.

Fremlin Bros of Maidstone were the leading brewers of Pale Ale in southern England and the main suppliers to Courages Brewery, the barrels being conveyed by barge to London. In 1891 Fremlins were employing more than 300 workers in the brewery. By 1892 Grants Morella Cherry Brandy had acquired a second distillery, together with an orchard of 20,000

95 *Floods in the area of the Medway bridge in 1878, one of numerous occasions on which parts of the town near the river were flooded.*

96   *Weeks Engineers, High Street.*

97   *View of Waterside.*

cherry trees at Lenham. The Medway Brewery, which had come under the control of A.F. Style in 1881, bought a number of public houses in north-west Kent, then merged with E. Winch of Chatham in 1899 and operated thereafter as Style & Winch. The brewery at Chatham was closed and production was centred in Maidstone.

By the end of the century Maidstone had several wholesalers able to compete with their London counterparts. Arkcolls had been grocers in Lower Stone Street since the 1820s, but by the 1870s they were engaged in the wholesale trade, even having a London warehouse. They employed up to 70 people and were possibly the largest importers in England of Dutch cheeses. Laurence's wholesale business followed much the same pattern. They, too, were large-scale cheese importers, and cured large quantities of bacon. Their employees were almost as numerous as those of Arkcolls. Marchant & Tubb were large wholesalers of drapery and clothing.

EIGHT

Major Changes in the Town and the First World War, 1900-1939

Despite the strong criticism by the Royal Commission of 1833 of electoral malpractices, these still continued. In 1900 the successful Liberal parliamentary candidate was found guilty of bribery carried out on his behalf by his agents. Twenty-five cases were discovered of bribes of 7s. 6d. or 10s. being given to electors, but this was evidently not regarded as a serious issue by those entitled to vote since a Liberal was returned with an increased majority at the ensuing by-election.

In 1892 the Maidstone authorities applied to the government for permission to install an electricity supply system. Permission was granted but there was a hiatus whilst the council consulted on how to proceed. In 1899 the Urban District Council took the decision to keep the undertaking within its own control, and a generating station was built on the Fair Meadow, near to the baths, the riverside wharf being convenient for the handling of coal. The works were finally opened and an electricity supply made available to customers in 1901, the year the Yeomanry returned from the Boer War.

The same year, and prior to any national legislation on the subject, Maidstone's education committee set up a schools medical service. The Education Act 1902 removed from local authorities the control of secondary schools and technical schools and passed it to county councils. Boroughs and urban districts, such as Maidstone, were left with control over primary schools. The council strengthened teaching in primary schools by replacing pupil-teachers with trained teachers. The number of fee-paying schools was reduced to two, and new, enlarged, schools were built at Tonbridge Road and Union Street. The former was almost twice the size of Heath Street school, which it replaced, and the latter was to accommodate 1,000 pupils. The council had hoped to develop junior technical classes in the Technical School but this concept was frustrated by the Board of Education. It was, however, able to set up a careers advisory and juvenile employment service for the benefit of former pupils of secondary schools.

By 1900 the geographical spread of the town necessitated a tramway system and authority for this was sought from the Board of Trade. At

The West Kent Yeomanry parading in the town on their return from the Boer War, 1901.

first this was refused, but in 1903 permission was given to run trams on just one route from the High Street to the town boundary on the Barming road. The wages of employees were fixed by the council at 4s., with 5s. a day for drivers and 3s. a day for conductors. The subject of how tram stops should be named was the cause of controversy, some favouring the adjacent streets and others the local public houses, but it was the latter proposal which prevailed.

Some 643 shops were listed in a town directory of 1903, an important development around the turn of the century being the introduction of branches of large London retailers into Maidstone. These provided stern competition for small shopkeepers. W.H. Smith,

the newsagents, had a stall at the East railway station, whilst Freeman, Hardy & Willis, the shoe makers, had shops in the High Street and Week Street. Boots, the chemists, the Maypole Dairy and the Home & Colonial Stores all had shops in Maidstone by this time. One of the firms listed in the directory is Garrett, Saveall & Co., which had become one of the largest engineering companies in the town, but there is no further reference to them after 1903 and it is possible that the company moved to some other part of the country, or simply went out of business.

W.A. Stevens, who were involved in mechanical and electrical work in St Peters Street, engaged with Tilling, the bus manufacturers of London, on

99 *Opening of tramway in High Street, 1904.*

100 *Tram in Tonbridge Road near Oakwood.*

101   *View of the High Street, 1896 (above).*

102   *Bodiam's Wheelwright and Signwriter's shop, Medway Street.*

103　George Mence Smith's shop in High Street, 1910.

104　King Bros' shop in the High Street (below), 1909.

105   *Another view of G.M. Smith's shop, showing the range of work undertaken and goods sold.*

the development of an electrically driven vehicle and this was in production by 1908. Chassis and engine were both Maidstone products, and Tilling-Stevens became one of the town's largest manufacturers. They built new works in St Peters Street in 1912 for the manufacture of fire engines and chassis for the East Kent Motor Company, and by 1920 they were employing around one thousand workers.

Consideration was given to extending the tramway system to other areas of the town but the Board of Trade refused to allow trams to run on Gabriels Hill and Week Street. It did agree that there should be an extension to Loose, and this was introduced in October 1907, whilst a further extension to Tovil was authorised in January 1908.

There were reductions in the number of drinking establishments in the town in the early years of the century and in 1908 Maidstone was left with 73 alehouses, 40 beerhouses and 48 beer off-licences, as well as a number of inns and taverns. There were also the private clubs, such as the Maidstone Club, those associated with the political parties, and working men's clubs, over which the town's authorities had only limited control.

106   *Bottom of Gabriels Hill, 1910.*

107   Middle Row.

108   Week Street County Club (below).

109   *Tonbridge Road Labour Club.*

The Bluecoat School in Knightrider Street was largely demolished in 1907 to make way for the Maidstone Baptist church and a car park. In 1908 a government inspector produced a critical report on church schools, and in particular the Wesleyan school, the performance of which he considered highly unsatisfactory. There appears to have been no improvement and the school was finally closed in 1910, despite strong opposition from the school managers.

The engineering firm of Jesse Ellis expanded its manufactures and its agency for hop cultivation machinery, but its road repair contracts with the County Council came to an end in 1904 and by

110   *Bluecoat School, Knightrider Street.*

1907 the firm was insolvent and forced to give up its St Peters Street works. Ellis continued

111   *Floods on Fair Meadow, 1909.*

with the manufacture of agricultural machinery elsewhere, but this too came to an end in 1910. At the same time his former works were taken over by Sharps.

Flooding continued to be a problem in the early 1900s. Maidstone's population had increased to 35,475 in 1911. Accommodation was principally in terraced houses, whether in working-class or more affluent areas, detached, or even semi-detached, houses being comparatively rare. The accession of King George V was celebrated in 1910. There is anecdotal, but almost certainly exaggerated, evidence of a diminution of crime in Maidstone

at this time, the *Kentish Express* reporting that 'crime in Maidstone was practically absent

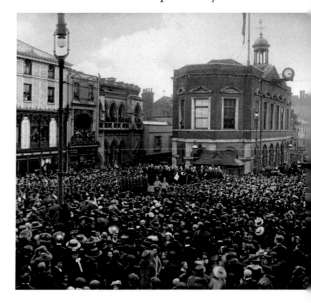

112   *Crowds in the High Street celebrating the accession of George V, 1910.*

proving the excellence of the police supervision'. Absences of pupils from school remained a problem on account of the widespread practice of employing children on farms, particularly at harvest time. The record of All Saints' primary school for 29 September 1912 reads, 'Re-opened school after hopping holidays. Attendance very bad, 111 absentees. Several farms in the area had not finished picking.'

Employment in local and national government offices was approaching a figure of 400 and transport was becoming an important employer in the town, the number engaged by 1911 being of the order of 1,350. Of these, 524 were in road transport and 361 on the railways. Employment on the Medway was declining but it still retained some importance.

In 1911 Sharps introduced what was to become their most famous product, 'Kreemy Toffee'. Two years later a large new factory employing some 300 workers was erected in St Peters Street, and in the following year the firm advertised for a further 100 female workers. The Rootes brothers made a substantial technological advance when, in 1912, they designed and manufactured the first Singer motor car. In later years they were to create the Rootes group, which became one of the town's major employers.

The County Council's education office was situated in London and was subject to much criticism, on the grounds both of its remoteness and its cost. The council had been urged to move the office to Maidstone in 1905 but declined to do so. In 1907 there were further widespread

113   *County Council buildings, County Road, 1914.*

demands that the office should be moved but these, too, resulted in no change. In 1910 the council finally agreed to build new offices in front of the Sessions House, which were completed in 1913, and provision was made to accommodate a Council Chamber.

The opening of the new County Council offices allowed for rationalisation in the location of the various council departments. Besides the education department's move, the county accountant and health departments, till then situated in various parts of the town, were centrally relocated. The exception was the county surveyor's department, which was located in purpose-built accommodation near to the River Medway with the advantage of a wharf and storage facilities for road building materials.

In 1912, at Cobtree Manor, Sir Garrard Tyrwhitt-Drake opened up for the public his private collection of animals, with admission costing 6d. or 3d. in the evening. In 1914 the enterprise was moved to Tovil Court and became the Maidstone Zoological and Pleasure Gardens. The outbreak of war caused the zoo to be closed in 1915. Under legislation allowing magistrates to close down what they deemed to be public houses superfluous to the needs of the town, Maidstone's licensing justices reduced the number of licensed premises to 106 by 1914. This was 20 fewer than there had been ten years earlier.

In the First World War Maidstone escaped aerial bombardment, although dogfights between British and enemy aircraft did take place overhead. Many thousands of soldiers and their horses were billeted in the town throughout the war, whilst war wounded were cared for at Hayle Place and the Howard de Walden Institute. Local industry was affected by the shortage of male labour. Tilling-Stevens broadened production to include the manufacture of munitions, and Weeks & Sons took on engineering contracts for the armed forces. Cliffords devised new uses for their hop-screens, which were adapted as camouflage for gun emplacements, and Drake & Fletcher adapted hop-spraying machines for use against gas attacks. Armstrongs of Week Street

114 *Sir Garrard Tyrwhitt-Drake was six times Mayor of Maidstone. He opened the private zoo at his home, Cobtree Manor, to the public in 1912. It was moved to Tovil Court two years later. Closed during the First World War, it re-opened at Cobtree Manor in 1933 but finally closed in 1959. Tyrwhitt-Drake gave his collection of carriages to the town in 1946 and left his manor to the public at his death in 1964. It was converted by the Council into a Museum of Kent Life.*

were contracted to provide khaki uniforms and built a factory for the purpose.

Steps were taken towards improving the health of mothers and children in 1916 when Mrs Bellairs, the wife of the Maidstone Member of Parliament, set up an infant welfare centre with the help of the Kent midwifery service. Although originally a voluntary organisation, in 1919 it was taken over and expanded by the council to include ante-natal units in Padsole and Medway Street. At about this time the council also appointed a number of health visitors.

The industrial, commercial and domestic customers who contracted for a supply of electricity increased gradually in number, so that by 1916 it had reached 1,043, but the largest consumer, by far, remained the electric tramways

undertaking. Brewing and hop growing were affected by the war. Shortages were occurring in the town's public houses and there was a fear that hop prices would collapse completely. A 50 per cent reduction was enforced on hop acreage and a Hop Control Committee to purchase all hops was set up under the chairmanship of George Foster Clark, who was appointed as Hop Controller. His appointment was evidence of the importance of Maidstone and its market to the hop trade.

In 1917 Sharps factory was employed in the pulping of fruit on a large scale, which was then sent to London to make jam for the army. The Agricultural Hall in Lock Meadow, which had opened in 1915, was commandeered as an army slaughterhouse and, then, as accommodation for

115   *The War Memorial in Broadway.*

116   Arrival of a convoy of wounded soldiers at Maidstone Station (1916), *by Frank Hyde* (PCF KTMM 17 007).

alien detainees. Much of the Corn Exchange was used for billeting troops although it remained possible for grain sales to continue.

Although many women were enjoying higher than usual incomes in what had previously been men's work, increased food prices were causing distress, and on occasion industrial action was taken in an effort to counter the effects. The papermakers' union demanded a war bonus from Reed's at Tovil, whilst similar demands at smaller mills, when rejected, led to a strike in April 1916. After this had endured for three weeks the employers gave in and agreed to an increase of 1s. a day for skilled workers and 6d. for others. To offset food shortages, in 1915 the council made more land available for use as allotments. A local Food Control Committee was formed in 1917, with representatives of labour on the committee,

but the Trades Council, representing Maidstone's trade unions, protested strongly at what it saw as butchers favouring richer customers. It urged that, in wartime, whenever vacancies arose on the council, its own nominees should fill some of the vacancies. The council was not prepared to agree to this, although it remained ready to co-opt Trades Council nominees to some of its committees.

Coal was in very short supply in the latter years of the war. The council set up a committee to negotiate prices with local coal retailers and 200 tons were purchased and stored in the Tithe Barn (the Archbishop's stables, now the Carriage Museum) for sale to the poor when the need arose.

The West Kent Federation of Women's Institutes, which was based in Maidstone, was

117 *The Weavers, St Faiths Street, original headquarters of the West Kent Federation of Women's Institutes.*

Large-scale housing provision became an urgent issue in the 1920s, and in 1921-2 some 224 council houses were erected on the Old Tovil Road. Two hundred government- and council-subsidised houses had been built by private builders by the mid-1920s. In 1921 the council acquired the site at Springfield which had once been the home of the Balston family, one of Maidstone's leading paper manufacturers, and used the premises to house the Education Department and the County Library. The library was reorganised, allowing open access to books, but was hardly a success, people preferring to utilise the commercial library run by Boots the chemists. Either its readers had greater access to newly published books or the choice of books catered better for popular tastes.

created in 1918. The Clare Recreation Ground was developed in 1922 on land donated by Sir Edward Sharp. Maidstone United Football Club resumed play in 1919 on a semi-professional basis but they were not a major force for long. Formal balls at the *Royal Star Hotel* (formerly the *Star Inn*), the Corn Exchange and the barracks were popular among the middle classes. In 1920 there were three cinemas in the town, the Empire Electric in Earl Street, the Popular Picture Palace in Pudding Lane, and the Central, built in that year, in King Street. The last of these boasted a restaurant, an organ and a seven-piece orchestra. The Palace Theatre had variety shows twice nightly. Using the powers granted by the 1904 Act, the justices had further reduced the number of public houses to 83 by 1920, but there were no further closures. Indeed, the number increased to 89 when the town boundaries were extended.

Several local companies engaged in the automobile trade had become widely, even nationally, known. During the 1920s the Rootes group developed into large-scale motor wholesalers and became the country's biggest motor retailer. The company also developed a charabanc on a Tilling-Stevens chassis at the works in Mill Street, but in 1928 transferred its head office to London and vehicle manufacture to other parts of the country. All that remained in Maidstone was the distribution and servicing of vehicles. Drake & Fletcher expanded to become agents for General Motors and other car manufacturers. Tilling-Stevens had also become a household name through the manufacture of its coach and commercial vehicles. Alabaster, Passmore & Co. at Tovil and Esgate, Chamberlain & Co. were both large printing firms, the latter engaging in box making in 1920.

In 1925 George Foster Clark's appointment as Hop Controller came to an end and he was

118   A view of Pudding Lane showing a public
house (later the Ritz Cinema), the Maidstone
Water Co., and Fremlin's offices, pre-1926 (above).

119   Palace Cinema, Gabriels Hill.

120   *The opening of the widened bridge, 1926. The cost of £53,000 was shared between the Ministry of Transport, Rochester Bridge Wardens and Maidstone Town Council.*

offered a knighthood, which he declined. He introduced a generous pension scheme for his employees in that year, salaried staff receiving half their salary at the time of retirement, whilst weekly paid men received 25s. a week and women 15s. Pensions were guaranteed for five years or for life, whichever was the later. In 1928 Foster Clark, whose products by now included not only custard powder but canned fruit, vegetables and soups, became a limited company and all employees with a minimum of ten years' service were given shares, the number based on their length of service.

Sharps remained the largest employer in the confectionery trade, with Jackson & Smith, the makers of 'Bettina toffee' being another sizeable undertaking. James Clifford, the longest-lasting manufacturer in the town, continued to produce rope, matting, sails and tarpaulin, and Armstrongs continued with clothing manufacture after their wartime contracts came to an end. The two furniture manufacturers of some size were S.P. Sanders in Boxley Road and R.W. Robson in Union Street.

The volume of traffic resulted in the bridge over the Medway being widened in 1926, and

121 *Bus Station, Palace Avenue, 1922.*

the capacity of the electricity generating station was expanded in 1928 to enable it to supply the whole of the town. The street lamps were lit by seven boys on bicycles who were paid 15s. a week. Their services were dispensed with in 1935 when time switches were installed. The tramway route to Tovil was replaced by motor buses in 1929 and the tramway system as a whole finally came to an end in 1930 when it was replaced by a trolley bus service to Loose and a new trolley bus route was introduced from the centre of town to Sutton Road.

Sir Garrard Tyrwhitt-Drake organised annual circuses and menageries in the Agricultural Hall until 1933, the proceeds going to local hospitals, but in that year he re-opened his zoo at Cobtree Manor, with an admission charge of 7d. for adults and 3d. for children.

As the county town, a garrison town, and with much in the way of both public and commercial employment, Maidstone continued to attract newcomers, and good transport links with London and the major Kentish towns encouraged commuters to move to the town. By 1931 the population had reached a figure of 42,280, approaching three times that of 1831, and in 1932 the borough boundaries were extended to include almost 6,500 acres in Malling, Hollingbourne and Maidstone rural districts.

122 *Maidstone Zoological and Pleasure Gardens, the lions.*

Slum clearance in Padsole and Upper Stone Street was begun in 1933 and flats erected in Ringlestone and, in 1936, behind King Street. The council encouraged house ownership by offering 20 year mortgages on 90 per cent of the cost of houses selling for £600 or less. In 1934 the council built 90 non-subsidised houses which were offered at cost price with 20 year mortgages fixed at 3.75 per cent. By the end of 1939 almost 2,000 council houses had been built, and in addition 760 subsidised houses were provided by private builders. The council had made, in total, some 650 loans to owner-occupiers.

New wings were added to the Sessions House in the years 1936 and 1939 and in 1939-40 the county police headquarters at Wren's Cross was replaced by new premises on the Sutton Road. By 1939 the County Council had become the largest single employer in Maidstone.

NINE

The Second World War to the Present Day

Maidstone barracks had a constantly changing military presence throughout the Second World War, whilst Mote Park became the venue for additional military encampments. The government viewed the Maidstone area as likely to be free from enemy air attack and at an early stage it was considered suitable as a centre for evacuees from London, despite warnings from the Town Council that the area was highly likely to be subject to attack. The town did, indeed, experience enemy bombing in the latter part of 1940. On one occasion it was hit by an enemy shell fired from France, and on another considerable damage was caused by the shooting down of an enemy plane.

Public buildings such as the museum, West Kent Hospital, the boys' grammar school and Maidstone East station suffered damage during the war, as did factories and shops, particularly those in Mill Street. Houses were destroyed or damaged by bombing, whilst a number of properties in Hardy Street were destroyed when a Messerschmitt aircraft was shot down. In 1944 there was some damage caused by flying bombs. The County Council set up rest centres

for those bombed out of their homes. In the course of the war 70 Maidstone residents were killed and 124 seriously injured as a result of enemy bombing.

Anti-invasion measures were introduced in south-east England in 1940 and one of the most important was the Medway defence line, which effectively used the river as an anti-tank ditch. So-called anti-tank nodal points were put in place at key road intersections and some were located in Maidstone, adjacent to the river.

The town's available workforce was depleted again as men and, to a lesser extent, women were called up or volunteered for service in the armed forces. Tilling-Stevens were engaged in the manufacture of searchlights and gyro compasses, and the reconditioning of aircraft engines. Rootes produced parts for aero engines in the earlier phase of the war but when it became clear that the town was open to enemy air attack the work was transferred elsewhere. The Maidstone works then concentrated on repairs to the bodywork of military vehicles. Cliffords were engaged in the manufacture of coconut matting for landing strips for small

123　*War damage to railway goods yard.*

124　*War damage to factory, Hart Street, 1944.*

aircraft and amphibious vehicles, and Alabaster Passmore carried out much government printing work, the most noteworthy contract being the Beveridge Report, which was to form the basis of the post-war welfare state.

As in the First World War, women took over much work that had previously been done by men, the Town Council persuading the Ministry of Health to provide day nurseries and the first nursery opening on London Road in December 1942. Maidstone's important industries of brewing, papermaking and food production were all affected by the conflict. Papermaking was hit by a shortage of wood pulp, much of which had been imported, and the government exercised overall control of food production, processing and distribution.

Beer was never rationed, but the need to give priority to supplies for the armed forces resulted at times in supplies for public houses being curtailed. Food supplies were managed by the Ministry of Food through the agency of local Food Control Committees, Maidstone having set up its committee in June 1939 when war appeared to be a distinct possibility. The public was urged to produce its own food as much as possible and land which had been earmarked for building purposes was made available for allotments. The council sold seeds to the public at cost price and allowed allotment holders to keep pigs and poultry. It used the greenhouses in publicly owned gardens to produce cucumbers and tomatoes for retail sale.

125 *Bomb damage, Mill Street, 1940. The naval officer driving the car escaped unharmed.*

126 *Tilling-Stevens factory, St Peter's Street.*

The government encouraged the provision of facilities for communal meals and the council introduced a canteen at the Corn Exchange capable of serving 400 people and staffed by the Women's Royal Volunteer Service. Meals were offered at a cost of 9d., tea costing 1d. The facilities were later designated British Restaurants. Meals were provided for schoolchildren by the Kent Education Committee from 1941 onwards.

In common with all other boroughs, Maidstone lost the responsibility for policing in 1943, and this was followed by the loss of control of primary educational facilities in 1944, which were passed to the County Council. The town remained almost unaffected by the Labour landslide in the 1945 General Election. Conservative domination continued, the party having last been defeated in a General Election by a Liberal in 1906, when Sir Alfred Bossom

('neither the one thing nor the other', as Winston Churchill once remarked) was elected by a comfortable majority.

After the war Sir Garrard Tyrwhitt-Drake offered to donate his collection of horse-drawn carriages to form the nucleus of a museum. His offer was accepted and the collection, later augmented by carriages from elsewhere, was housed in the stables located opposite the Archbishop's Palace.

The Town Council lost control of electricity and gas supplies when the government nationalised these industries in 1947 and 1948 respectively. The small generating station at Lockmeadow continued to be used for a time by the nationalised electricity industry. Provision of services ancillary to medicine, such as assistance to expectant mothers and day nurseries, or TB and VD clinics, had been fairly progressive, but in 1948 these were largely absorbed into the National Health Service, maternity and child welfare becoming the responsibility of the County Council.

Although the town lost direct control of certain functions it gained increased employment opportunities as the county town became home to the district offices of nationalised services. Employment was further augmented by the enlarged facilities of the Kent Fire Service at its new headquarters in Tovil and by the offices of the Kent County Constabulary headquarters on Sutton Road. In 1950 Tilling-Stevens ceased to exist as such, being taken over by Rootes, but Drake & Fletcher expanded, having acquired an agency for Jaguar cars.

In 1948 Sir Alfred Bossom MP presented the town with a finial from the bomb-damaged House of Commons. In 1950 the new Maidstone Technical Institute opened at Oakwood Park and in the following year Shepway County and Junior schools were built with facilities for more than 1,000 children. The population had increased to 54,035 by 1951 but there were significant changes in the pattern of employment. By comparison with figures from some 20 years earlier, the number of males employed in manufacturing declined from 36 to 34.7 per cent, in transport from 11.9 to 8.8 per cent, and in agriculture and extractive industries from 5.7 to 2.4 per cent (the figure having been as high as 8.5 per cent in 1911), whilst those engaged in personal service

127   Finial rescued from the House of Commons, Brenchley Gardens.

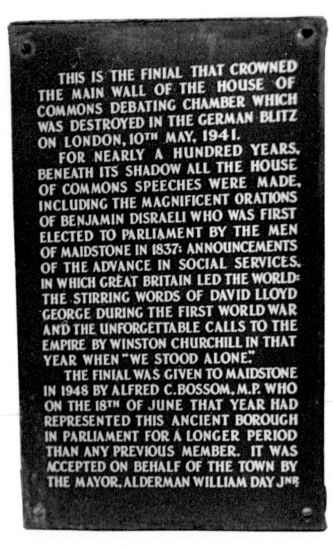

THIS IS THE FINIAL THAT CROWNED THE MAIN WALL OF THE HOUSE OF COMMONS DEBATING CHAMBER WHICH WAS DESTROYED IN THE GERMAN BLITZ ON LONDON, 10TH MAY, 1941.

FOR NEARLY A HUNDRED YEARS, BENEATH ITS SHADOW ALL THE HOUSE OF COMMONS SPEECHES WERE MADE, INCLUDING THE MAGNIFICENT ORATIONS OF BENJAMIN DISRAELI WHO WAS FIRST ELECTED TO PARLIAMENT BY THE MEN OF MAIDSTONE IN 1837: ANNOUNCEMENTS OF THE ADVANCE IN SOCIAL SERVICES, IN WHICH GREAT BRITAIN LED THE WORLD: THE STIRRING WORDS OF DAVID LLOYD GEORGE DURING THE FIRST WORLD WAR AND THE UNFORGETTABLE CALLS TO THE EMPIRE BY WINSTON CHURCHILL IN THAT YEAR WHEN "WE STOOD ALONE."

THE FINIAL WAS GIVEN TO MAIDSTONE IN 1948 BY ALFRED C. BOSSOM, M.P. WHO ON THE 18TH OF JUNE THAT YEAR HAD REPRESENTED THIS ANCIENT BOROUGH IN PARLIAMENT FOR A LONGER PERIOD THAN ANY PREVIOUS MEMBER. IT WAS ACCEPTED ON BEHALF OF THE TOWN BY THE MAYOR, ALDERMAN WILLIAM DAY JNR.

128 *Plaque by the House of Commons Finial.*

fell from 3.1 to 1 per cent. In service industries and commerce the figure increased from 30.1 to 35.1 per cent, and in building from 9.1 to 11 per cent. In the case of female employment there was a massive drop in the numbers engaged in personal service, from 34.5 to 7.5 per cent, whilst in manufacturing there was an increase from 22.2 to 24.2 per cent, and in the service industries and commerce a large increase from 40.2 to 62.4 per cent.

The lack of house building during the war years, and the numbers of families occupying unsuitable accommodation in the wartime huts which had once housed soldiery in Mote Park and on the Boxley Road, gave rise to an urgent need for additional housing. The council played a major role, providing 1,000 houses between the end of the war and February 1951, a significant proportion of them on the Shepway estate. With the sole exception of Brighton, no other council in the south east built as many. In broadly the same period, private enterprise provided 264 houses, which included prefabricated properties, an emergency form of post-war housing.

129 *Distribution of tins of dripping sent from New Zealand for Maidstone residents, 1948.*

Food shortages persisted in the immediate post-war years and anything which alleviated these was welcomed. Foster Clark had difficulties dealing with post-war competition as pre-prepared foods became popular with the public. The company purchased a pasta manufacturing business in Manchester and machinery was installed in Maidstone for canning Kentish fruit and vegetables.

The Corn Exchange had been a popular venue for dances in the 1920s and '30s, but by 1955 these had largely gone out of fashion and the premises were converted to a municipal theatre which was renamed the Hazlitt Theatre (Hazlitt having been minister at the Week Street Independent Congregation which, as the Unitarian Chapel, remains close by).

The Ritz (previously known as the Popular Picture Palace, and later the Pavilion) was burned down in 1954. The Central, which was owned by the same company, Associated British Cinemas, was also damaged by fire in the following year. The owners decided to build a new cinema on the site of the Central in King Street and call it the Ritz and this opened in 1957. The Palace in King Street, which had converted from theatre to cinema in 1931, had closed by this time but was re-opened for the period during which the new Ritz was being built. When that work was completed the Palace finally closed, and it was demolished in 1960. In 1957 the Empire (named at first the Medina and then the Regal) was also closed.

130 *Hazlitt Theatre in Earl Street was formerly the Corn Exchange.*

131   *Regal Cinema, Earl Street.*

When sweet rationing ended in 1953, Sharps reintroduced many of their pre-war lines. Barley sugar sweets were made for the royal family and the firm was appointed a Warrant Holder to the Queen in 1960, but it became expedient to merge with Robertson & Woodcock, the manufacturers of 'Trebor' confectionery. Findlater, Mackie & Co., wine and spirit merchants and a subsidiary of Fremlins, purchased George Prentis & Co. Ltd., a similar Maidstone company, in 1959 and the name of the merged company became Findlater, Prentis.

As had been perceived as early as 1929, the growing population of Maidstone and, in particular, the stream of lorries passing through the town on the way to the important communications centres of Ashford and Dover resulted in traffic congestion. The council had envisaged a by-pass for the town but approval from the Ministry of Transport and the County Council was delayed and work had not commenced at the outbreak of war. The traffic situation had worsened by the latter part of the 1950s, exacerbated by Maidstone's development as a regional shopping centre. In 1960-1 the first stretch of what was to become the M20 was eventually commenced as a Maidstone by-pass. The A20(M), as it was designated, commenced at what is now junction 5 of the motorway and terminated at junction 7. From 1963 this obviated the need for through traffic to pass through the centre of the town on the A20. In a further move to ease congestion on Maidstone's roads the Borough Council erected the town's first multi-storey car park in Medway Street.

132   *Granada Cinema, Lower Stone Street.*

The ill-health of Sir Garrard Tyrwhitt-Drake during 1959 led to the closure of the zoo which he had created and opened to the public. On his death in 1964 the Cobtree estate which he owned was bequeathed for the benefit of the people of Maidstone and was, in part, converted to a golf course and country park. By 1961 cinemas were unable to compete successfully with newer forms of entertainment and only two remained of the five which had been in existence in 1945.

Masons Waterside brewery was taken over by Shepherd Neame of Faversham in 1960 and then closed down. The Medway brewery, having been taken over by Courage, suffered the same fate in 1964. Fremlins, the one major Maidstone brewery which remained independent of the larger London brewers, embarked on a major rebuilding in the late 1950s and early 1960s. The furniture manufacturers which existed pre-war had all gone out of business by 1960 although

a more recently established company, Len Ltd, was flourishing at its Water Lane factory. The one firm which had been in existence in the town, certainly, since the very early 1800s, and probably before that, was James Clifford and Son, and by the 1960s it had diversified from hop bagging, rope and twine to floor coverings and travel goods. Jackson & Smith had moved from confectionery manufacture to wholesale grocery by 1960, and, on the retail side, enterprises such as the Sainsbury supermarket on Gabriels Hill and branches established by the Co-operative movement were offering ever more serious competition to the small shopkeepers of the town.

The boundaries of the borough had been extended in 1954 to include the civil parishes of Boughton Monchelsea and Otham, and by 1961 the population of the expanded borough had reached 59,790. Many commuters were travelling

133   *Courage Brewery, St Peter's Street, 1974.*

134   *A bird's eye view of industrial Maidstone.*

135 *View of Shepway Estate, c.1960.*

to work elsewhere, largely to London, but there were some 5,000 travelling into Maidstone on each working day. In the 1950s the council continued with their major house-building programme and by 1961 the Shepway estate numbered 2,409 houses, Shepway Ward having grown in size by then to encompass a little more than a quarter of the town's entire population. The council also began work on a project for more than 400 houses at Park Wood on the outskirts of the town.

Foster Clark's trading position continued to decline and the company was taken over by St Martin's Preserving Company in 1960, but by 1965 the business went into receivership prior to being bought out by Oxo, which continued with Foster Clark products within its own organisation.

In 1964 an enlarged County Library was opened at Springfield. The trolley bus service to Shepway came to an end in 1967 and was replaced by motor buses, and in the same year Rootes was taken over by the American Chrysler Corporation. Fremlins ceased to function as an independent brewery and was taken over by Whitbread in 1967, although brewing was to continue at the Maidstone premises for some years yet. Drake & Fletcher continued to make agricultural machinery, but engineering in Maidstone on any significant scale was nearing an end. Those firms which had been engaged over the years in the production of engineering products were now principally concerned with the retail motor trade. W. Weeks & Son closed down their agricultural machinery works in Maidstone in early 1967 and transferred their

136   *National Provincial Bank, High Street.*

plant to Rye in Sussex. They failed to prosper there and the firm ceased to trade in 1971.

Bank mergers resulted in the creation of the National Westminster Bank, but that part of the merged organisation which included what, many years before, had been the Kentish Bank (but which had, from 1918, been part of the National Provincial Bank) reverted, within the new group, to an earlier title, the Kentish Bank Office. Style & Winch was taken over by Barclay Perkins in 1929, but the parent company allowed it to continue brewing in Maidstone under its own name until, in 1971, it was closed down by Courage who had become its new owner.

In 1964/5 the Maidstone and District Council of Churches conducted a review of social services in Maidstone, not in any scientific manner but by way of interviews with all statutory and voluntary organisations concerned with the provision of services, as well as with many individuals. A report entitled *Maidstone: a Closer Look* was published in November 1965, when vagrancy remained something of a problem in the town:

> There is an alarming number of people in the Maidstone area who are 'living rough' because they have no roots in the community anywhere. In particular, it is estimated that a score or more make their beds in the vicinity of the Old Palace every night and many more vagrants are to be observed sleeping at intervals along the river bank on either side of the town, both by day and night.

The population reached 70,987 in 1971, increasing in the decade from 1961 by 11,197, and additional housing was needed. In the ten years following the end of the war the council had been the principal provider of new housing in the town, but this was now to change. Private house building went ahead rapidly, mainly on the outskirts of the town, but also by infilling or by small-scale developments. By 1971 just over one half of housing in the borough consisted of owner-occupied dwellings, with less than 30 per cent being rented council property and less than 20 per cent private rented housing. A decade previously only 44 per cent had been owner-occupied.

Maidstone United Football Club had, to a limited extent, become a professional side in the early decades of the century and it continued to be so until 1939. After the war it reverted to being an amateur club, and as such it had some success in the mid-1950s. Thereafter it languished until 1971, when it became a professional side once more, playing in the Alliance Premier League. It now plays in the Ryman League.

The electricity generating station on Lockmeadow was finally demolished in 1975. Whitbread allowed the Fremlin brewery to continue operations after taking over the company, but finally closed the brewhouse in September 1972. It was demolished in 1976 and, not long after, so were the other parts of the brewery. What remained was used as offices and for storage. Maidstone's first multiple shopping centre, the Stoneborough Centre (later renamed the Chequers Centre), was built between King Street and Gabriels Hill during the period 1964-6.

Local government reorganisation in 1974 resulted in the Borough Council being merged with the Rural District Council, as a result of which the reconstituted Borough Council held jurisdiction over a considerably extended area of the surrounding countryside. Its functions remained largely unchanged although, in common with borough councils throughout the land, it lost its aldermen and the link with the jurats of Tudor times was thus broken.

Turkey Mill had been sold in 1794 to the Hollingworth brothers, and when William Pitt, the last member of the family to be the sole director of the company, died in 1976, it was bought by Wiggins Teape, who closed down the mill and transferred production to Stoneywood, near Aberdeen. Thus 280 years of continuous papermaking at Turkey Mill came to an end, a record matched by no other British paper mill. The Young family purchased the site and moved to Turkey Court from where they operated a car business.

137 *E.B. Copnall's 'The Stag', originally located in Stag Place, London, is now installed in the River Park.*

In the last decades of the 20th century and the first decade of the 21st, apple orchards were grubbed out and replanted with smaller trees so that fruit picking no longer needed the use of ladders. Many hop grounds were grubbed out, too, as foreign competition became intense. More car parking facilities were made available in the town centre but parking remained a problem. The County Council took over Invicta House, adjacent to Sessions House, as additional office accommodation in 1983, and new law courts were built by the riverside in the West Borough. Maidstone Hospital was opened in 1983 at Hermitage Lane, Barming, and the headquarters of the Maidstone and Tunbridge Wells NHS Trust was located there. The West Kent Hospital and the Opthalmic and Aural Hospital were then closed. In the year 2000 work commenced on the creation of a Millennium River Park.

Barclays Bank in the High Street was closed and converted to a wine bar, and the *Royal Star Hotel* was demolished and the site converted

138   *Royal Star Arcade, High Street entrance.*

to a small shopping centre, Royal Star Arcade. A much larger development was that on the old Fremlins brewery site, where a shopping centre, Fremlin Walk, with 800 parking spaces and some fifty shops covering 350,000 square feet was built. Many small office premises were either built anew or converted from existing buildings, whilst large office blocks, such as the Ministry of Agriculture in Sittingbourne Road and the printing works in Tovil, were demolished and housing built on their sites.

The town has become an important centre of local and county government, as well as one of the most important commercial shopping centres in the county of Kent.

139   *Main entrance to Fremlin Walk, with earlier brewery clock.*

140   *Part of Fremlin Walk shopping area.*

141   *Fremlin Walk car park seen from across the river.*

BIBLIOGRAPHICAL NOTE

There are many references to Maidstone in *Archaeologia Cantiana*, vols 1 – present-day, which are available in the main Kent public libraries. See the index to each volume or the collective indices published from time to time in the series. Alternatively, the complete collection of volumes is contained on one DVD which can be purchased from the Kent Archaeological Society.

Maidstone Corporation and the earlier Burghmote records, as well as Maidstone wills, are in the Centre for Kentish Studies, Maidstone. Probate inventories and church court records are in Canterbury Cathedral Library and Archives. Miscellaneous material concerning the town can be found in various series of records at The National Archives. Copies of newspapers (some series incomplete) are held at the British Library, Colindale, whilst the *Maidstone Gazette* and *Maidstone Journal* are held on microfiche in some Kentish Libraries. The Centre for Kentish Studies and Maidstone Reference Library have useful information on poor relief; the former has more on primary and secondary education. For primary sources, a useful guide to locations can be found in Field, J. et al, *West Kent Sources*, 3rd edition, North West Kent Family History Society (1998).

BIBLIOGRAPHY

PRIMARY SOURCES

Poll Books, Maidstone.

Anon., *A Relation of the Proceedings at the Election of Burgesses for Maidstone* (London, 1701)

Bulteel, J., *A Relation of the Troubles of the Three Foreign Churches in Kent* (London, 1645)

Copley, G.J. (ed.), *Camden's Britannia – Kent, 1586* (London, 1977)

Gilbert, W.B., *The Accounts of the Corpus Christi Fraternity* (Maidstone, 1865)

Hearne, E.T. (ed.), *Edulphus, Textus Roffensis, c.975* (Oxford, 1720)

James, W.R., *The Charters and other Documents Relating to the King's Town and Parish* (London, 1825)

Martin, K.S. (ed.), *Records of Maidstone, being Selection of Documents in the Possession of the Corporation* (Maidstone, 1926)

Morgan, F. (ed.), 'Maidstone' in *Domesday Book – Kent, 1086* (Chichester, 1983)

Pratt, J., Stoughton, J., *John Foxe, The Acts and Monuments, vol. 6, 1659* (London, 1877)

Swinnock, G., *The Life and Death of Mr Thomas Wilson* (London, 1672)

NEWSPAPERS AND DIRECTORIES

Maidstone Journal (1786-1911)
Maidstone Gazette (1815-1851)
Maidstone Gazette (1902-1982)
Kent Messenger (1859-date)
Maidstone & Kent County Standard (1875-1912)
Bailey's British Directory (London, 1874)
Pigot's London & Provincial Directory (1828-9)
Kelly's Directorate of Maidstone and Neighbourhood (1947)

SECONDARY SOURCES

Anon., *Maidstone, A Closer Look; A Review of Social Services in a Prosperous County Town* (Maidstone & District Council of Churches, 1965)

Anon., *Industries of Maidstone* (Maidstone, 1881)

Armstrong, A., *The Economy of Kent, 1640-1914* (Woodbridge, 1995)

Balston, J.N., *The Elder James Whatman, England's Greatest Papermaker 1702-1759* (West Farleigh, 1992)

Balston, T., *William Balston, Paper Maker 1750-1849* (London, 1954)

Boorman, H.R.P., *Pictures of Maidstone, the County Town of Kent* (Maidstone, 1965)

Bourner, M., Hull, F., Tate, R. (eds.), *History of Bearsted and Thurnham* (Bearsted & Thurnham History Book Committee, n.d.)

Brandon, P., Short, B. (eds.), *The South-East from AD 1000* (Harlow, 1990)

Brown, R.J., *Old Houses and Cottages of Kent* (London, 1994)

Cave-Browne, J., *The History of the Parish Church of All Saints, Maidstone* (Maidstone, n.d.)

Clark, P., *English Provincial Society from the Reformation to the Revolution; Religion, Politics and Society in Kent 1500-1640* (Hassocks, 1978)

Clark, P., Murfin, L., *The History of Maidstone; The Making of a Modern County Town* (Stroud, and Maidstone Borough Council, 1995)

Cleggett, D.A.H., *History of St Michaels and All Angels* (n.p., n.d.)

Cope, H.J., *Maidstone Grammar School 1549-1949. A Record* (Maidstone, 1949)

Craig, F.W.S., *British Parliamentary Election Results 1918-49* (Chichester, 1983)

Defoe, D., *A Tour thro' the whole island of Great Britain*, 1798 (London, 1971)

Detsicas, A., *The Cantiaci* (Gloucester, 1983)

Digby, D., Adams, M. (eds.), *West Kent within Living Memory* (Newbury and West Kent Federation of Women's Institutes, 1995)

Dobson, B., 'The Monks of Canterbury in the Later Middle Ages, 1220-1540, in Collinson, P., Ramsey, N., Sparks, M. (eds), *A History of Canterbury Cathedral* (Oxford, 1995)

Dobson, R.B., *The Peasant's Revolt of 1381* (London, 1970)

Drewitt, P., Rudling, D., Gardiner, M., *The South-East to AD1000* (London, 1988)

Du Boulay, F.R.H., *The Lordship of Canterbury* (London, 1966)

Edwards, E.P., *Maidstone in 1992* (Brighton, 1992)

Everitt, A., *The Community of Kent and the Great Rebellion 1640-1660* (Leicester, 1966)

Fearnside, W.G., *Tombleson's Thames and Medway, Picturesque Views engraved on Steel by the First Artists*, c.1830 (London, 1980)

Fiennes, C., *The Illustrated Journeys of Celia Fiennes, 1685-c.1712* (Stroud, 1995)

Goodsall, R.H., 'Maidstone Industry and Trade' in *A Third Kentish Patchwork* (Harrietsham, 1970) 'Water Borne Trade on the Medway' in *A Fourth Kentish Patchwork* (Harrietsham, 1974)

Green, I., *Maidstone: A Pictorial History* (Chichester, 1988)

Grove, L.R.A., 'Newark, Maidstone' in Detsicas, A., *Collectanea Historica, Essays in Memory of Stuart Rigold* (Maidstone, 1981)

Hales, I., 'Maidstone's Water Supply' in *Bygone Kent*, vol. 4., November 1983; 'Prisons', vol. 4, October 1984; 'Police', vol. 4, December 1984; 'Zoo', vol. 5, February 1985; 'Typhoid Epidemic', vol. 5, April 1984; 'Theatres, Live and Electric', vol. 7, July 1986; 'Sharp's Kreemy Toffee Story', vol. 7, May/June 1986; 'Rootes', vol. 7, October/November 1986; 'George Foster-Clark and the Eiffel Tower Works', vol. 10, March 1989; 'Markets and Fairs', vol. 10, August 1989

Hales, I., *Old Maidstone, A Selection of Postcards from the early Years of the Century*, vol. 1 (Rainham, 1980) *Old Maidstone, A Selection of Postcards from the early Years of the Century*, vol. 2 (Rainham, 1980) *Old Maidstone, A Selection of Postcards from the early Years of the Century*, vol. 3 (Rainham, 1988) *Old Maidstone Public Houses in Postcards and Photographs* (Rainham, c.1982)

Harris, V., *The Story of Maidstone Zoo* (Rainham, 1994)

Harvey, J.M.W., *Jack Cade's Rebellion of 1450* (Oxford, 1991)

Hasted, E., *A History and Topographical Survey of the County of Kent*, vol. 3, 1790, with Introduction by A. Everett (Maidstone, 1972)

Hemming, B., 'Maidstone' in *The House of Commons, 1660-1690* (London, 1793)

Hills, R.M. (ed.), *Studies on the History of Papermaking in Britain* (Aldershot, 1993)

Hilton, J., *Maidstone: An Outline History* (Hadlow, 1979)

Hobsbawm, E.J., Rudé, G., *Captain Swing* (London, 1969)

Jeal, R., *Maidstone Baptist Church 1838-1984* (n.p., n.d)

Jessop, F.W., *A History of Kent*, 1958 (Chichester, 1974)

Jones, J.G., *A Political Tour through Rochester, Chatham, Maidstone, Gravesend, &c.*, reprinted with 'Introduction' by P. MacDougall (Rochester, 1997)

K.C.C. Education Committee, *Maidstone Technical High School for Boys 1918-1968* (Maidstone, 1968)

Knighton, K.L., *Three Hundred Years of Religious Freedom, 1662-1962* (Maidstone, 1962)

Lampreys, S.C., *A Brief Historical and Descriptive Account of Maidstone and its Environs* (Maidstone, 1834)

Lansberry, F., *Government and Politics in Kent, 1640-1914* (Woodbridge, and K.C.C., 2001)

Lawrence, M., *The Encircling Hop; A History of Hops and Brewing* (Sittingbourne, 1990)

Lawson, T., Killingray, D. (eds), *An Historical Atlas of Kent* (Chichester, 2004)

Lewis, P.W., 'Changing factors of location in the papermaking industry as illustrated by the Maidstone Area', in *Geography*, vol. 52 (1967)

Livingstone, H., *Around Maidstone, Francis Frith's Photographic Memories* (Salisbury, 1999)

Loades, D.M., *Two Tudor Conspiracies* (Cambridge, 1935)

Maidstone and District and East Kent Bus Club, *Fleet History of Maidstone Corporation 1904-74* Aylesford, 1975)

Maidstone Choral Union, *Fifty Years of Singing, a short history of the Maidstone Choral Union* (Maidstone, 1953)

Melling, E., *History of Kent County Council* (Maidstone, 1975)

Melling, E., Grove, L.R.A. (eds), *Memories of Maidstone* (Maidstone, 1987)

Moss, J., *Public Assistance in Kent 1930-48* (Maidstone, 1951)

Namier, L., Brooke, J., *The House of Commons 1754-90* (London, 1964)

Newman, J., 'Maidstone' in *West Kent and the Weald*, 2nd edition (Harmondsworth, 1976)

Newton, W., *History and Antiquities of Maidstone, the County town of Kent* (Maidstone, 1741)

Osborn, T., *The History of the Mote Cricket Club 1857-1951* (Maidstone, 1990)

Phillips, J.A., 'Municipal Politics in Later-Eighteenth century Maidstone', in Hellmuth, E., *The Transformation of Political Culture. England and Germany in the Later Eighteenth Century* (Oxford, 1990) 'From Municipal Matters to Parliamentary Principles: Eighteenth-century Borough Politics in Maidstone', in *Journal of British Studies*, vol. 27 (1988)

Philp, B., 'Maidstone's Great Palace, 1988-92' in *Archaeology in the Front Line, 50 Years of Kent Rescue 1952-2002* (Dover, 2002)

Powell, E., Trevelyan, G.M., *The Peasant's Rising and the Lollards* (London, 1899)

Preston, J.M., *Industrial Medway: an Historical Survey* (Rochester, 1977)

Russell, J.M., *The History of Maidstone*, 1881 (Rochester, 1978)

Scotney, D.J.S., *The Maidstone Trolleybus 1928-67* (London, 1972)

Smith, A.W., *Wesleyan Methodist Church. A Short History of the Maidstone Circuit* (Maidstone, n.d.)

Streatfield, S., *The History of Maidstone Grammar School* (Oxford, 1915)

Thomas, B.G., *Firefighting in Maidstone* (Maidstone, 1976)

Topping, M., *The Church of St Francis, Maidstone. A Narrative History 1880-1980* (Maidstone, n.d.)

Watts, M., *The Dissenters, From the Reformation to the French Revolution* (Oxford, 1978)

Whitehead, R.A., *Jesse Ellis and the Maidstone Wagons* (Tonbridge, 1992)

Whyman, J., 'The Kentish Portion of an Anonymous Tour of 1809', in Detsicas, A., Yates, N. (eds), *Studies in Kentish Modern History* (Maidstone, 1983)

Woods, T.P.S., *Prelude to Civil War 1642; Mr Justice Malet and the Kentish Petitions*, 'Introduction' by Roots, I. (Salisbury, 1980)

Worssam, B.C. et al, *Geology of the Country around Maidstone* (London, 1963)

Wright, C., *Kent through the Years* (London, 1975)

UNPUBLISHED WORKS

Geary, H.V.R., *Graham's Illustrated Guide to Maidstone and Neighbourhood* (Maidstone, 1884), text in Maidstone Reference Library

Williams, K.V.C., 'Elementary Education in Maidstone 1903-1932'. MA thesis, University of London, 1978

INDEX

Note: Numbers in **bold** refer to illustrations